总主编 文 旭

NEW WORLD
INTERACTIVE ENGLISH

新世界

交互英语视听说 2 学生用书

主　　编：孙　阳
副主编：廖　颖
编　　者：（按姓氏笔画顺序）
　　　　　王　霞　刘建芳　何　姗
　　　　　张一颖　赵丽娜　胡登攀
　　　　　曾　苹

原版主编：Rob Jenkins
原版作者：Martin Milner
　　　　　Kristin L. Johannsen
　　　　　Rebecca Tarver Chase

清華大学出版社
北 京

Copyright © 2017 by National Geographic Learning, a Cengage company.
Original edition published by Cengage Learning. All Rights reserved.
本书原版由圣智学习出版公司出版。版权所有，盗印必究。

Tsinghua University Press is authorized by Cengage Learning to publish and distribute exclusively this adaptation edition. This edition is authorized for sale in the People's Republic of China only (excluding Hong Kong SAR, Macao SAR and Taiwan). Unauthorized export of this edition is a violation of the Copyright Act. No part of this publication may be reproduced or distributed by any means, or stored in a database or retrieval system, without the prior written permission of the publisher.
本改编版由圣智学习出版公司授权清华大学出版社独家出版发行。此版本仅限在中华人民共和国境内（不包括中国香港、澳门特别行政区及中国台湾）销售。未经授权的本书出口将被视为违反版权法的行为。未经出版者预先书面许可，不得以任何方式复制或发行本书的任何部分。

"National Geographic", "National Geographic Society" and the Yellow Border Design are registered trademarks of the National Geographic Society® Marcas Registradas.

Cengage Learning Asia Pte. Ltd.
151 Lorong Chuan, #02-08 New Tech Park, Singapore 556741
本书封面贴有 Cengage Learning 防伪标签，无标签者不得销售。

北京市版权局著作权合同登记号　图字：01-2016-8548

版权所有，侵权必究。举报：010-62782989，**beiqinquan@tup.tsinghua.edu.cn**。

图书在版编目（CIP）数据

新世界交互英语. 视听说学生用书. 2 / 文旭总主编；孙阳主编. —北京：清华大学出版社，2017.3（2021.8重印）
ISBN 978-7-302-46289-7

Ⅰ. ①新… Ⅱ. ①文… ②孙… Ⅲ. ①英语—听说教学—高等学校—教材 Ⅳ. ①H319.39

中国版本图书馆 CIP 数据核字（2017）第 021465 号

责任编辑：刘细珍
封面设计：子　一
责任校对：王凤芝
责任印制：丛怀宇

出版发行：清华大学出版社
网　　址：http://www.tup.com.cn，http://www.wqbook.com
地　　址：北京清华大学学研大厦 A 座　　　邮　编：100084
社 总 机：010-62770175　　　　　　　　　　邮　购：010-62786544
投稿与读者服务：010-62776969，c-service@tup.tsinghua.edu.cn
质量反馈：010-62772015，zhiliang@tup.tsinghua.edu.cn

印 装 者：山东临沂新华印刷物流集团有限责任公司
经　　销：全国新华书店
开　　本：210mm×285mm　　印　张：9　　字　数：253 千字
版　　次：2017 年 3 月第 1 版　　　　　　　印　次：2021 年 8 月第 9 次印刷
定　　价：58.00元

产品编号：071650-04

PREFACE

　　《国家中长期教育改革和发展规划纲要（2010—2020年）》明确指出，要"适应国家经济社会对外开放的要求，培养大批具有国际视野、通晓国际规则、能够参与国际事务和国际竞争的国际化人才"。《大学英语教学指南》提出，"大学英语课程应根据本科专业类教学质量国家标准，参照本指南进行合理定位，服务于学校的办学目标、院系人才培养的目标和学生个性化发展的需求"。

　　《新世界交互英语》是清华大学出版社站在国家外语教育与人才培养的战略高度，从美国圣智学习出版公司引进优质原版素材、精心打造出版的一套通用大学英语教材。为满足国内大学英语教学的实际需要，出版社邀请国内多所大学，在《大学英语教学指南》的指导下，对原版教材进行了改编。本套教材汇集全球顶尖品牌教学资源，贯彻启发性教学理念，以课堂教学为纽带，将全球化视野与学生真实生活联系起来，注重学生个性化发展需求，力求培养具有较高英语应用能力和跨文化交际能力的国际化人才。

一、教材特色

　　本套教材主要有以下特色：

❶ 素材来源：汇集全球顶尖品牌教学资源

　　本套教材的素材源自全球两大顶尖品牌教学资源：美国国家地理（National Geographic Learning）和TED演讲（TED Talks），为学生提供了大量原汁原味的视频、音频和图片，将世界各地的自然风光、风土人情、文化习俗带进课堂，以拓展学生的思维，并拓宽他们的国际化视野，从而达到提高学生语言应用能力和跨文化交际能力之目的。

❷ 编写理念：倡导启发性教学

　　本套教材将全球真实事件和精彩观点引入教学，结合中国传统文化和国情，注重思维训练，启发思考，以帮助学生理解中西文化差异，在培养学生听说读写译等英语应用能力的同时，着力培养其国际视野和创新精神，实现学生的全面发展。

❸ 核心目标：用课堂连接世界与学生生活

　　本套教材以课堂教学为纽带，将多姿多彩的世界万象与触手可及的学生生活连接起来，让学生具有全球化视野的同时，关注自身生活，思考中国问题，并学会用英语去表达自己的思想，从而成长为兼具扎实英语基本功和敏锐批判性思维的国际化人才。

二、改编思路

中方编写团队在对原版教材进行本土化改编过程中，做了适当的增补、替换和删减等工作。主要改编思路如下：

❶ 增补中国文化和中国国情内容

本教材注重培养学生对中国传统文化的认同，着力培养学生使用英语介绍中国文化的能力。在问题设计、练习改编方面重视本土问题，以帮助学生理解中西文化差异；在翻译、写作、口语活动中融入文化对比的元素，启迪学生对本土文化进行思考，培养其国际视野和中国情怀。

❷ 设计实用型和兴趣型练习

在设计练习时，适当参考了雅思、托福、大学英语四六级考试的题型，补充了更多的听力、翻译等练习，增强了教材的实用性；同时，结合时代发展，我们在"读写译"系列中加入扫描二维码以获取更多主题阅读材料的新元素，以充分调动学生的学习兴趣和求知欲望，使他们在主动学习的过程中提高英语水平和综合素养。

❸ 引入批判性思维训练和创新写作题型

本教材注重引导学生正确区分人物与观点、事实与解释、审美与判断、语言与现实、字面义与隐含义等，对问题进行批判性评价。"读写译"系列教材每个单元专门设计了一项针对批判性思维训练的练习，根据阅读模块内容启迪学生深度思考，进而提出独到见解；在写作能力培养上，设计了环环相扣、逻辑紧密的练习，体裁题材多样，积极鼓励创新写作，实现批判思维与创新写作的结合。

三、教材结构

本套教材分为"视听说"和"读写译"两个独立系列，每个系列包含学生用书和教师用书各四个级别。每个级别包含八个单元，每个单元可供四课时使用。

其中，"视听说"每个单元包含两大部分。第一部分主要围绕音频素材展开，包含A、B、C、D四个板块，分别对应四个教学目标（Goals）。第二部分的E、F两个板块主要包括视频素材和拓展练习，每个单元均包含美国国家地理录像视频Video Journal和拓展练习Further Practice，每两个单元之后含一个TED Talks视频。

"读写译"每个单元包含Reading、Writing和Translation三个部分。Reading部分包含两篇课文；Writing部分介绍若干个Writing Skills；Translation部分包含汉译英和英译汉两个篇章翻译练习。每个单元最后都设计了Weaving It Together综合和拓展板块，用以培养学生课下自学能力。

四、适用对象

本套教材适用于我国高校各层次公共英语和英语专业基础技能课程教学，同时也适用于成人自学。

五、编写团队

本套教材的总主编为西南大学文旭教授。"视听说"1-4册主编分别为莫启扬、孙阳、李成坚、段满福；"读写译"1-4册主编分别为崔校平、姜毓锋、刘瑾、马刚。来自全国近十所高校的几十名专家和骨干教师参与了本套教材的设计和编写，美国圣智学习出版公司的英语教育专家和教材编写专家对全书进行了审定。

在改编之前，我们广泛咨询了国内外英语教育领域的资深专家学者，开展了充分的调研和分析，确定了本套教材的改编理念和方案，最终使本套教材得以与广大师生见面。教材的改编凝聚了诸多专家学者的经验和智慧。在此，对为本套教材的改编和出版付出辛勤劳动的所有老师以及出版社的各位同仁表示衷心的感谢。由于水平有限，不足之处在所难免。我们真诚地希望大家提出宝贵意见，并在未来的修订中使之更趋完善。

文旭

2017年2月

UNIT WALK-THROUGH

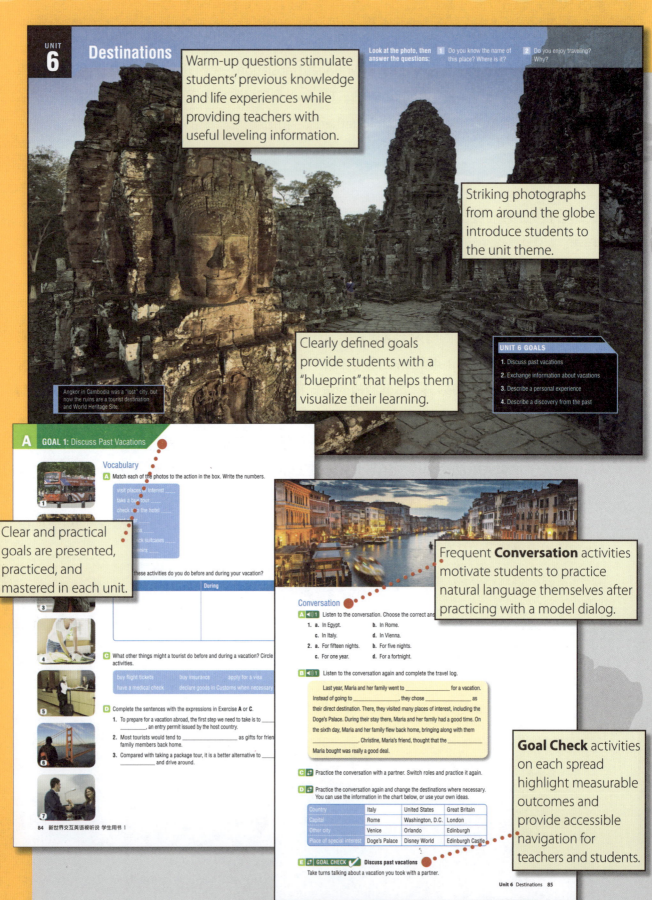

B GOAL 2: Exchange Information About Vacations

In **Lesson B** students develop their oral skills through a natural progression of aural language input, pronunciation, and open-ended communication.

Orlando
Orlando is a city in Florida in the United States. It is a major tourist destination, with an estimated 57 million tourists visiting each year. They come to Walt Disney World, Sea World, Universal Studios Florida, a large number of golf courses, and one of the biggest shopping malls in the United States. The city also has several important art museums. The population is around 250,000 people, with about 2 million people in the metro area.

Listening

A 🔊 2 Listen to the conversation. Choose the correct answer.
1. Chen is telling his friend about _____.
   a. his vacation b. his work c. his hobby d. his likes and dislikes
2. His friend is _____.
   a. bored b. interested c. tired d. worried

B 🔊 2 Listen to the conversation again. Circle **T** for *true* or **F** for *false*.
1. Chen went to Oklahoma. T F
2. He visited five theme parks. T F
3. He didn't like Sea World. T F
4. He went to the Spider-Man™ ride. T F
5. He visited Islands of Adventure. T F
6. He didn't try the Incredible Hulk Coaster. T F

Pronunciation: Reduction of *have to, has to, got to*

Pronunciation exercises give students item-specific practice with reductions, stress, rhythm, intonation, and minimal pairs.

A 🔊 3 Listen to the pronunciation of *have to, has to,* and *got to*. Notice how they sound like *hafta, hasta,* and *gotta* in fast speech.
1. I've **got to** finish my homework. (sounds like /gɑ-/)
2. He **has to** clean the house. (sounds like /hæ-s-/)
3. Do you **have to** work tomorrow? (sounds like /...

B 🔄 Practice these sentences with a partner. Pay a... of *have to, has to,* and *got to*.
1. Sorry, I have to leave now. 5. He h...
2. I've got to apply for a visa. 6. Do y...
3. Rosa has to pack her suitcase. 7. You'...
4. They've got to stay after class. 8. Tom...

86 新世界交互英语视听说 学生用书 1

Students gain confidence and develop their speaking skills with guided **Communication** activities.

Communication

A 🔄 Read the travel blogs below. Fill in the blanks with the past tense of the verbs in parentheses.

From Zanzibar to Zebras
Africa » Tanzania » Dar es Salaam » Zanzibar » Arusha   Read full story | Subscribe

December 12th, 2016
Day 1 _Arrived_ (arrive) in Dar es Salaam. _____ (check) into hotel. _____ (unpack) suitcases. Went swimming.
Day 2 _____ (take) boat to the island of Zanzibar.
Days 3–5 _____ (sunbathe) on the beach. _____ (go) diving.
Day 6 _____ (fly) to Arusha. Saw Kilimanjaro. It's BIG!
Days 7–10 _____ (take) a safari tour. _____ (see) hundreds of wild animals. Took lots of photos.
Day 11 _____ (return) to Arusha. _____ (buy) souvenirs. Took plane to Dar es Salaam and then flew home. Great trip.

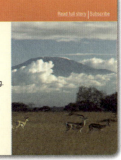

Mexico: Beaches and Pyramids
Mexico » Mexico City » Cancun » Tulum » Merida   Read full story | Subscribe

December 18th, 2016
Day 1 _Arrived_ (arrive) in Mexico City. _____ (take) subway to Chapultepec Park. _____ (go) to zoo.
Day 2 _____ (rent) a car. _____ (visit) the Pyramid of the Sun.
Days 3–5 _____ (fly) to Cancun. _____ (go) to the beach.
Day 6 Visited ruins at Tulum. _____ (watch) traditional dance show.
Day 7 Colonial city of Merida. Took a bus tour of the city. _____ (drink) hot chocolate in market.
Day 8 _____ (return) to Mexico City. Flew home.

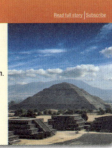

B 🔄 Choose one blog. With a partner, take turns asking each other questions about your vacation.

Where did you go next?   What did you do?   How long did you stay there?   Did you enjoy it? Why?

C 🔄 **GOAL CHECK** ✓ Exchange information about vacations
Join another pair of students. Tell them about your partner's vacation from Exercise **B**.

Unit 6 Destinations 87

Unit Walk-Through   v

UNIT WALK-THROUGH

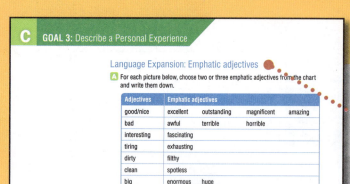

Language Expansion sections focus on specific areas that help students build language strategies and become more competent users of English.

Word Focus boxes provide definitions of additional vocabulary, useful collocations, and special usage.

Real Language information boxes in every unit focus students' attention on frequently used phrases and how to use them.

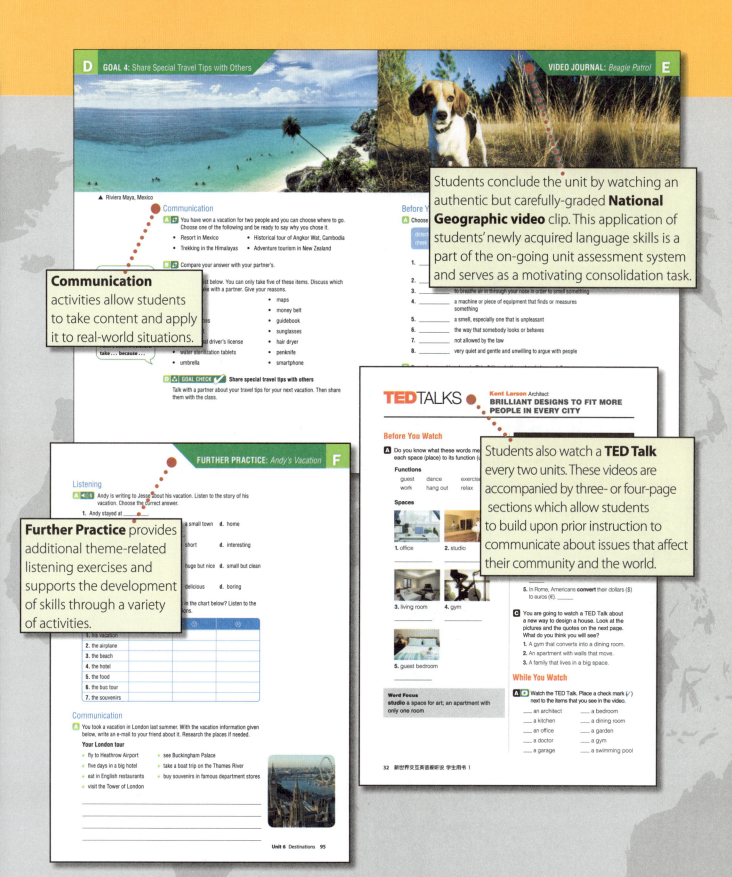

CONTENTS

	Unit Goals	Vocabulary
UNIT 1 — Moving Forward — Page 2	• Talk about plans • Discuss long- and short-term plans • Make weather predictions • Discuss the future	Short- and long-term plans Weather conditions Weather-specific clothing
UNIT 2 — Lifestyles — Page 16	• Give advice on healthy habits • Compare lifestyles • Ask about lifestyles • Evaluate your lifestyle	Healthy and unhealthy habits Compound adjectives

TEDTALKS Video Page 30 **Eralic Whitacre: A Virtual Choir 2000 Voices Strong**

	Unit Goals	Vocabulary
UNIT 3 — Achievements — Page 34	• Talk about today's chores • Interview for a job • Talk about personal accomplishments • Discuss humanity's greatest achievements	Chores Personal accomplishments
UNIT 4 — The Body — Page 48	• Discuss ways to stay healthy • Talk about lifestyles • Suggest helpful natural remedies • Explain cause and effect	Human organs Parts of the body Everyday ailments

TEDTALKS Video Page 62 **Lewis Pugh: My Mind-shifting Qomolangma Swim**

Listening	Speaking and Pronunciation	Video Journal	Further Practice
General listening: A talk show **National Geographic:** "Future Energy"	Talking about weekend plans Discussing the weather Reduced form of *going to*	**National Geographic:** "Solar Cooking"	"Education for Tomorrow: An Interview with Professor Adam Kwan"
General listening: Personal lifestyles **National Geographic:** "The Secrets of Long Life"	Discussing healthy and unhealthy habits Asking and telling about lifestyles *Should, shouldn't*	**National Geographic:** "The Science of Stress"	"How Long Will You Live?"
Listening for general understanding and specific details: A job interview **National Geographic:** "Humanity's Greatest Achievements"	Interviewing for a job Catching up with a friend Reduced form of *have*	**National Geographic:** "Spacewalk"	"Amazing Achievements: Stephen Hawking"
Focused listening Discussions: Different lifestyles **National Geographic:** "Tiny Invaders"	Talking about food and exercise that are good for you Suggesting easy remedies Linking with comparatives and superlatives	**National Geographic:** "The Human Body"	"In the Death Zone of Mount Qomolangma"

CONTENTS

	Unit Goals	Vocabulary
UNIT 5 Express Yourself — Page 66	• Talk about personal experiences • Make small talk with new people • Use small talk to *break the ice* • Learn to overcome a language barrier	Culture, communication, and gestures Small talk
UNIT 6 Cities — Page 80	• Describe your city or town • Explain what makes a good neighborhood • Discuss an action plan • Make predictions about cities in the future	City life Maps

TEDTALKS Video Page 94 **Diana Reiss, Peter Garbriel, Neil Gershenfeld, Vint Cerf: The Interspecies Internet? An Idea in Progress**

	Unit Goals	Vocabulary
UNIT 7 Consequences — Page 98	• Talk about managing your money • Make choices on how to spend your money • Talk about cause and effect • Evaluate money and happiness	Personal finance Animals Animal habitats
UNIT 8 Challenges — Page 112	• Talk about facing challenges • Discuss past accomplishments • Talk about abilities • Describe a personal challenge	Physical and mental challenges Phrasal verbs

TEDTALKS Video Page 126 **Michael Norton: How to Buy Happiness**

Listening	Speaking and Pronunciation	Video Journal	Further Practice
General listening Conversations: Small talk **National Geographic:** "Taking Pictures of the World"	Talking about what you have or haven't done Making small talk *Have* or *has* vs. contractions	**National Geographic:** "Orangutan Language"	"Drinking Tea, Breaking the Ice"
General and focused listening A radio interview: Jardin Nomade in Paris **TED**TALKS "How Food Shapes Our Cities"	Discussing good and bad elements in a neighborhood Predicting the future of cities Emphatic stress	**National Geographic:** "Fes"	"Forests for Cities"
Listening for specific details: At a travel agency Listening for key information **TED**TALKS "Michael Norton: How to Buy Happiness"	Making decisions about spending money Talking about important environmental issues Intonation, sentence stress	**National Geographic:** "The Missing Snows of Kilimanjaro"	"Enjoy a Nature Vacation!"
General listening An interview: Jenny Daltry, herpetologist **National Geographic:** "Arctic Dreams and Nightmares"	Discussing challenges Talking about abilities Words that end in *–ed*	**National Geographic:** "Searching for the Snow Leopard"	"How Do You Spell…"

Moving Forward

UNIT 1

As global trade has increased, port cities like Singapore have become more and more important.

Look at the photo, then answer the questions:

1 Why do you think shipping ports are important?

2 Are you looking forward to the future? Why?

UNIT 1 GOALS

1. Talk about plans
2. Discuss long- and short-term plans
3. Make weather predictions
4. Discuss the future

A GOAL 1: Talk About Plans

Vocabulary

A Number the pictures to match the phrases from the box.

1. study for the next test	4. buy a new car	7. buy my own house
2. get a new job	5. have children	8. speak English fluently
3. do the laundry	6. clean the house	

B Write the plans from Exercise **A** in the correct column.

> I need to buy a new car. My car is really old.

> I don't want to have children now. I'm too young.

Short-term plans	Long-term plans

C Write your short-term and long-term plans in the table below. Number the plans in order of importance to you (1 for the most important plan). Compare your list with a partner's. Give reasons.

Short-term plans	Long-term plans
○	○
○	○
○	○
○	○
○	○

Conversation

A 🔊 1 Listen to the conversation. Choose the correct answer.

1. a. How to study for a test.   b. The dirty cloth.
   c. A fun party.   d. How to spend the weekend.
2. a. Studying.   b. Doing the laundry.
   c. Going to the beach.   d. Having a test.

B 🔊 1 Listen to the conversation again and fill in the blanks.

Mai: Hi, Kiri. What are you going to do _____?

Kiri: Well, I'm going to _____ and _____. Why? Why do you ask?

Mai: We're going to _____. Do you want to come?

Kiri: Mmm, I'm not sure. I'd love to, but… you know… work.

Mai: Come on. It's going to _____!

Kiri: Well, maybe I can _____ tonight. And I can _____ when we come back.

Mai: So you're going to come?

Kiri: Sure!

> **Real Language**
> We can say *Mmm* or *I'm not sure* to show uncertainty.

> When/Where/How/Why are you going to . . . ?

C Practice the conversation with a partner. Switch roles and practice it again.

D **GOAL CHECK** ✓ **Talk about plans**
Tell a partner your plans for this weekend.

> I'm going to go hiking this weekend.

Unit 1 Moving Forward 5

B GOAL 2: Discuss Long- and Short-Term Plans

Listening

A 🔊 2 Listen to the interview with a pop singer. Is he talking about his short-term plans or long-term plans?

B 🔊 2 Listen again and circle **T** for *true* or **F** for *false*.

1. Pedro is going to record his new album in June.	T F
2. You can buy Pedro's new album in stores.	T F
3. Pedro is going to take a break in the summer.	T F
4. Pedro is going to do a world tour this year.	T F
5. Alicia is going to have a baby in July.	T F
6. The baby isn't going to change Pedro's life.	T F
7. Pedro is going to start making a film at the end of the year.	T F

C 🔄 Practice the conversation with a partner. Switch roles and practice it again.

Pronunciation: Reduced form of *going to*

A 🔊 3 Listen and repeat.

B 🔊 4 Listen to the sentence and check (✓) the correct box.

	Full form	Reduced form
1. When are you going to finish?	☐	☐
2. They're not going to like it.	☐	☐
3. We're going to leave at three thirty.	☐	☐
4. I'm going to take a shower.	☐	☐
5. Are you going to take a taxi?	☐	☐
6. What are you going to do this weekend?	☐	☐
7. I'm not going to go to the meeting.	☐	☐
8. When is Saleh going to arrive?	☐	☐

C 🔄 Take turns reading the sentences in Exercise **B** with either the *full form* or the *reduced form*. Your partner has to say which form you used.

For Your Information
Life changes from having children

According to experts, having a baby, especially a first baby, changes many aspects of one's life. It can cause pressure in the relationship with one's partner and may require change and adjustment in both parents' career goals. It can have both positive and negative effects on friendships, as well as affecting relationships with your own parents and your in-laws. It even brings changes in people's identity and sense of who they are.

A hang glider soars above Yosemite National Park in the United States.

Communication

A What are your short-term and long-term plans? Check (✓) the correct column.

Short-term plans			
Are you going to . . .	Yes, I am.	I'm not sure.	No, I'm not.
eat out tonight?			
go to a party this weekend?			
play or watch a sport this evening?			
rest this weekend?			

Long-term plans			
Are you going to . . .	Yes, I am.	I'm not sure.	No, I'm not.
start your own business?			
learn another language?			
move to another country?			
buy a new car?			

B With a partner, take turns asking and answering the questions in Exercise **A**. Then ask a *Wh-* question.

C **GOAL CHECK** ✓ **Discuss long- and short-term plans**

Tell a partner your plans for tonight and your plans for the next five years. Use the words in the box to help you.

> Are you going to start your own business?

> Yes, I am.

> What type of business?

> I'm not sure. Maybe a hang gliding school.

tomorrow	next weekend
next week	next month
next year	in five years

Unit 1 Moving Forward 7

C GOAL 3: Make Weather Predictions

Language Expansion: Weather conditions

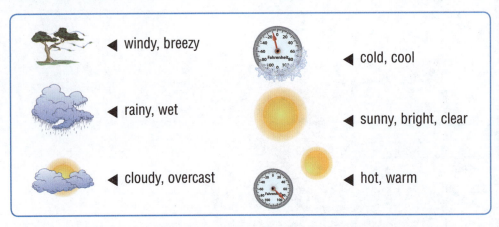

We use adjectives to describe the weather. Today is **sunny** and **warm**.

A What's in the picture? Fill in the blanks with correct words.

B Complete the sentences. Use the words on this page.

1. It's not going to rain tomorrow. You don't need to take your _____ or your _____.

2. Put on your sweater. It's going to be _____ outside.

3. The weather forecast says it's going to be cloudy today. You don't need to take your _____.

4. It's going to be _____ and _____ tomorrow, so don't forget your sun hat.

C Take turns asking and answering the questions about weather with a partner.

1. Which do you like better, hot weather or cold weather? Why?

2. What's your favorite season and why?

3. Do you think weather affects the way people feel?

Conversation

A 🔊 5 Listen to the conversation. Choose the correct answer.

1. a. Rain forest.   b. Umbrella factory.
   c. Airport.   d. Seaside.
2. a. It's going to be sunny.   b. It's going to rain.
   c. It's going to snow.   d. It's going to be cloudy.
3. a. The man and woman almost have everything ready for the trip.
   b. The man and woman will go to the seashore together.
   c. The woman doesn't know that the weather is hot.
   d. The woman will probably take her beach umbrella.

B 🔊 5 Listen to the conversation again and fill in the blanks.

Andrew: Do we have everything ready for _____?
Barbara: Sure. Everything's ready.
Andrew: Do you think it's going to _____?
Barbara: No, they say it's going to _____.
Andrew: Are you going to take _____?
Barbara: No, I said it's going to _____. It's not going to _____.
Andrew: No, I mean your _____.
Barbara: Oh, I see. Yes, that's a good idea.

C Practice the conversation with a partner. Switch roles and practice it again.

D GOAL CHECK ✓ **Make weather predictions**

Talk to a partner. What is the weather like now? What is it going to be like tomorrow?

Unit 1 Moving Forward   9

D GOAL 4: Discuss the Future

Listening

A Discuss the questions with a partner.
1. What are fossil fuels?
2. What is alternative energy?

B 🔊 6 Listen to the passage. Circle **T** for *true* or **F** for *false*.

1. Today, the world uses 320 million kilowatt-hours of energy a day.   T   F
2. In the long run, we need more renewable energy rather than fossil fuels.   T   F
3. A field in Germany produces enough energy for 33,500 homes.   T   F
4. The cost on satellites used to be high.   T   F
5. According to the passage, solar power is the best of alternative energy source.   T   F

C 🔊 6 Listen to the passage again and answer the questions.

1. How much energy will we need in 2100?
   _____
2. What are three problems with solar power?
   _____
3. What are two problems with wind energy?
   _____

D How do you think people will get energy in the future? Solar, wind, fossil fuels, or another way? Discuss these questions with a partner.

Word Focus

alternative something different

cost-effective something *cost-effective* saves money

renewable something you can use again and again

For Your Information   Renewable energy facts

- Enough sunlight falls on the earth's surface in one hour to meet the world's energy demands for a whole year.
- More than 300,000 homes added solar power in 2013, with the number of installations expected to reach 362,000 by 2016.
- Albert Einstein won the Nobel Prize in 1921 for his work on producing electricity from sunlight.
- One wind turbine produces enough electricity for 300 homes.
- People in China used wind power to grind grain in 200 BCE.
- To produce wind power, the wind must blow at least 14 mph (20 kph).

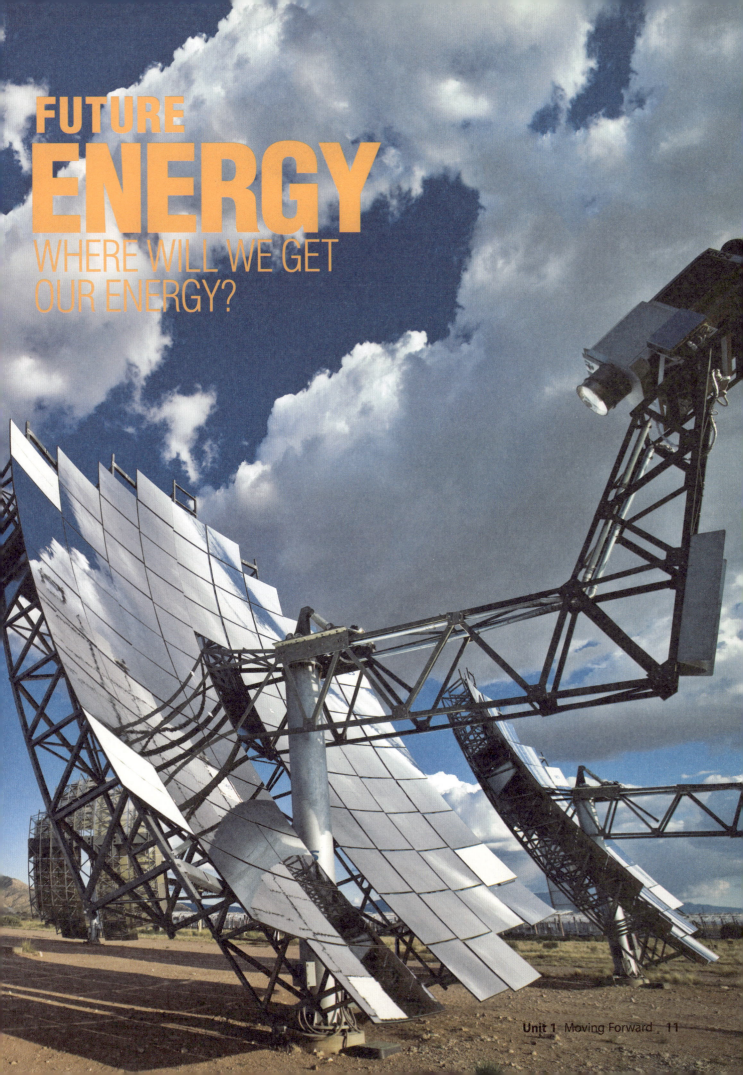
FUTURE ENERGY
WHERE WILL WE GET OUR ENERGY?

D GOAL 4: Discuss the Future

The surface of Mars

Communication

A Write more questions in the chart. Fill in the first column with your answers, and then ask your partner the questions. Compare and discuss your answers.

In the future, do you think . . .	Me			Partner		
	Yes	Maybe	No	Yes	Maybe	No
1. . . . people will live under the sea?						
2. . . . there will be enough food for everyone?						
3. . . . we will find a cure for cancer?						
4. . . . most houses will have solar panels?						
5. . . . people will travel to Mars?						
6. . . . wars will end?						
7.						
8.						

B  **Discuss the future**

Join two or three other students and discuss your ideas about the future.

VIDEO JOURNAL: Solar Cooking   E

solar cooking

▲ gas   ▲ electricity   ▲ firewood   ▲ solar energy

▲ wind

Before You Watch

A Look at the pictures. Discuss the questions with a partner.

1. What fuels can you use to cook food?
2. What fuel do you use to cook food?

B Write the meaning of the words with the help of a dictionary.

Borrego Springs: _____   consistency: _____

charcoal: _____   texture: _____

microbiologist: _____   attendees: _____

deforestation: _____   waterborne: _____

choke: _____   pasteurize: _____

While You Watch

A Watch the video. Check (✓) the correct box.

Benefits of solar ovens	Health	Environmental
1. You don't have to cut down trees.	☐	☐
2. African women don't have to walk a long way to collect firewood.	☐	☐
3. There is no smoke.	☐	☐
4. Solar ovens can be used to make water clean.	☐	☐
5. Solar ovens don't cause pollution.	☐	☐

Unit 1 Moving Forward

E | VIDEO JOURNAL: Solar Cooking

For Your Information
Solar cooking

There are many different types of solar cookers—more than 65 different designs are available today, and people are inventing their own variations every day. All of them work in similar ways. Some kind of reflective material concentrates sunlight in a small cooking area, where a black surface turns the light into heat. A clear material lets light enter but keeps the heat inside, so it can cook the food. Solar cooker projects are being carried out around the world. For example, in Lesotho, in southern Africa, women have started bakeries that use solar ovens. In Sudan, refugees in camps make their own solar cookers from local materials. And in India, entire villages have started cooking all their food in solar ovens.

B ▶ Watch the video again and choose the correct answer.

1. What does Eleanor Shimeall use to cook food?
   a. Gas.   b. Sun.   c. Wood.   d. Electricity.

2. Which is NOT mentioned in the video?
   a. African women have to walk a long way to collect wood.
   b. African women have to use wood to tend the fire.
   c. The smoke from the fire burns African women's eyes.
   d. Many African women died of lung cancer.

3. According to the World Health Organization, how many people died from smoke from wood fires each year?
   a. 2 million.   b. 22,000.   c. 22 million.   d. 2,000.

4. If people want to make water safe to drink, which of the following is NOT the solution?
   a. Boiling the water.
   b. Adding medicine to clean the water.
   c. Pasteurizing the water.
   d. Heating the water to 149 Fahrenheit.

5. What's the goal of Solar Cookers International?
   a. To protect African people.
   b. To cure the disease in Africa.
   c. To increase the use of solar cookers everywhere.
   d. To pasteurize solar cooker.

After You Watch

A With a partner, make a list of what you need to make a solar oven. Write instructions on how to make the oven. Use drawings if needed.

Communication

A With a partner, role-play the following situation.

Student A
You are running a workshop in Africa. You have to explain the benefits of using solar ovens. Some of the participants have doubts.

Student B
You are a participant in the workshop. Your mother cooked with wood and you cook with wood. You have doubts about changing. Ask questions.

FURTHER PRACTICE: *Education for Tomorrow: An Interview with Professor Adam Kwan* **F**

Listening

A 🔊 7 Listen to the passage and find out what Professor Kwan makes predications about? Circle the correct answers.

| homework | universities | classrooms | textbooks | computers |
| jobs | grades | lessons | tests | science classes |

B 🔊 7 Listen to the passage again and circle **T** for *True* or **F** for *False*.

1. The biggest change will be the cost of education.   T   F
2. Students will take classes over the Internet.   T   F
3. Students will mail their homework to their teacher.   T   F
4. People will spend less time studying.   T   F
5. People will keep the same job for their whole life.   T   F
6. People of different ages will go to school together.   T   F
7. Children will use tablets when they are six years old.   T   F
8. Foreign languages won't be very important.   T   F

C Talk about your predictions for schools in the future with a partner. Talk about the buildings, the teachers, the classes, the tests, and your other ideas.

UNIT 2
Lifestyles

A fisherman stands in a wooden boat on calm water. Below his boat, baitfish shine in the waters of the Dampier Strait in Indonesia.

Look at the photo, then answer the questions:

1. What does the photo show about the fisherman's lifestyle?
2. What is your lifestyle like? Can you improve it?

UNIT 2 GOALS

1. Give advice on healthy habits
2. Compare lifestyles
3. Ask about lifestyles
4. Evaluate your lifestyle

A GOAL 1: Give Advice on Healthy Habits

Vocabulary

Alicia has a healthy lifestyle. She's in good shape because she works out at the gym every day. She eats healthy food, like fresh fruits and vegetables.

Robert doesn't have a good lifestyle. He's in bad shape because he never gets any exercise. He eats too much junk food, so he's overweight.

A Complete the sentences with the words in blue.

1. I need to exercise more. I'm in _____.
2. Helen doesn't have a _____ diet. She eats a lot of junk food.
3. I have a healthy _____. I don't smoke and I exercise regularly.
4. I need to change my diet. I eat too much _____.
5. Jane is looking much better. She _____ and eats healthy food, like vegetables and fruit. Soon she'll be in _____.

B Write the activities in the correct column in the chart below.

▲ cycling

▲ smoking

▲ watching lots of TV

▲ drinking lots of water

▲ getting eight hours of sleep every night

▲ sunbathing

▲ eating a balanced diet

▲ eating lots of sugar

Healthy	Unhealthy

Conversation

A 🔊 1 Listen to the conversation. Choose the correct answer.

1. a. He is too fat.
   b. He has some health problems.
   c. His clothes are very tight.
   d. He has a long vacation.

2. a. Change his diet.
   b. Buy some bigger clothes.
   c. Ride a bike everyday.
   d. Eat more vegetables.

> **Real Language**
>
> We use *like what?* to ask for an example. We can use *like* to give an example.

B 🔊 1 Listen to the conversation again and fill in the blanks.

Alex: I need to _____. My clothes don't _____ anymore. What should I do?

Faisal: Well, instead of watching TV all day, you could _____.

Alex: _____?

Faisal: Like cycling, or you could work out at the gym.

Alex: I don't have time. I'm too busy.

Faisal: OK. Then you could _____. Eat something _____, like fruit.

Alex: You mean, no more hamburgers! Oh no!

Faisal: OK. Buy _____ then.

C Practice the conversation with a partner. Switch roles and practice it again.

D **GOAL CHECK** ✓ **Give advice on healthy habits**

Ask your partner questions about the activities in Vocabulary **B**. Then give your partner advice.

> **Do you get eight hours of sleep every night?**
>
> No, I don't.
>
> **You should get more sleep.**

B GOAL 2: Compare Lifestyles

▲ Ben

▲ Maggie

▲ Anita

Listening

A Look at the photos. Guess who is healthy or unhealthy. Rank the people from healthy lifestyle to unhealthy lifestyle. Compare your answers with your classmates. Listen and check.

Healthy lifestyle ←——————————————————→ Unhealthy lifestyle

B 2 Listen again and answer the questions.

1. Does Ben exercise every day?
2. Does Ben smoke?
3. What exercise does Maggie do?
4. Name two things that Maggie has for breakfast.
5. Where does Anita get her vegetables?
6. What is Anita's one bad habit?

C Work with a partner. What advice would you give to Ben, Maggie, and Anita on how to improve their lifestyles?

Pronunciation: *Should, shouldn't*

A 3 Listen to the sentences. Notice the difference between *should* and *shouldn't*.

I **should** get more sleep.   They **shouldn't** eat junk food.

B 4 Listen to the conversations and circle *should* or *shouldn't*.

Conversation 1
Lorena: What can I do to improve my image?
Zuleja: Well, you (should | shouldn't) change your hairstyle. Your hair looks great!
Lorena: And what about my clothes?
Zuleja: I think you (should | shouldn't) buy some more fashionable clothes. You (should | shouldn't) wear less makeup as well.

Conversation 2
Bill: What can I do to change my image?
Adrian: I think you (should | shouldn't) shave your beard, but you (should | shouldn't) change your hairstyle.
Bill: And what about my clothes?
Adrian: You (should | shouldn't) buy some new clothes.

C Choose one of the conversations and practice with a partner.

Fresh vegetables are part of a healthy diet.

Communication

A Answer the questions for yourself. Then survey two classmates.

Lifestyle choices	Me	
Do you play computer games?	Yes→No	_____ hours per day
Do you eat fresh vegetables?	Yes→No	_____ per day
Do you spend time on social media?	Yes→No	_____ hours per day
Do you work out every day?	Yes→No	_____ hours per day
Do you drink coffee or tea every day?	Yes→No	_____ cups per day
Do you eat sugary foods?	Yes→No	_____ per day

Classmate 1 Name _____		Classmate 2 Name _____	
Yes→No	_____ hours per day	Yes→No	_____ hours per day
Yes→No	_____ per day	Yes→No	_____ per day
Yes→No	_____ hours per day	Yes→No	_____ hours per day
Yes→No	_____ hours per day	Yes→No	_____ hours per day
Yes→No	_____ cups per day	Yes→No	_____ cups per day
Yes→No	_____ per day	Yes→No	_____ per day

> Ramona and I never play computer games, but Alfredo plays for about two hours per day.

> Yahir eats five pieces of sugary food per day and never works out. Salma has a much better lifestyle.

> Salma works out in the gym every day for two hours and doesn't eat sugary foods.

B Tell a partner about you and the classmates you interviewed.

C Tell your group about your lifestyle.

D **GOAL CHECK** ✓ **Compare lifestyles**

As a group, decide who has the best lifestyle and give reasons.

Unit 2 Lifestyles 21

C GOAL 3: Ask About Lifestyles

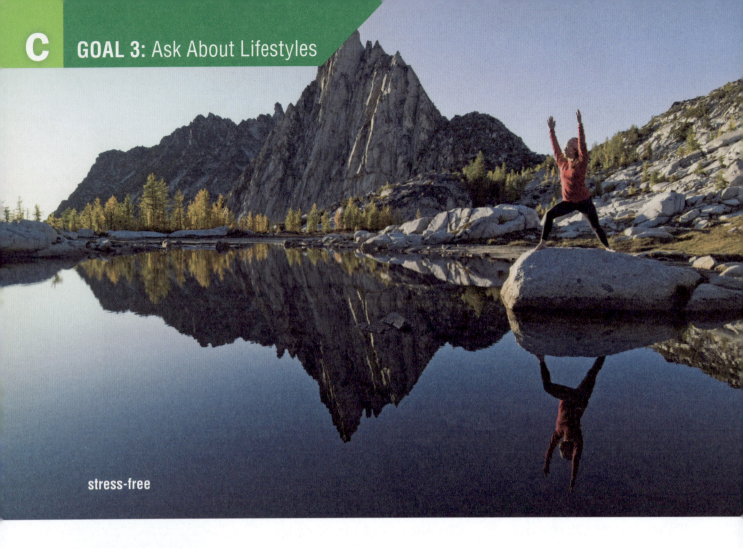

stress-free

a. works too much
b. delicious
c. without worries or problems
d. not high in calories
e. makes you happy
f. produced in your own garden
g. all your life
h. not made in a factory

Language Expansion: Compound adjectives

A Match the compound adjectives with their meanings.

1. mouth-watering _____
2. homemade _____
3. heartwarming _____
4. lifelong _____
5. stress-free _____
6. homegrown _____
7. overworked _____
8. low-calorie _____

B Complete the sentences. Use adjectives from Exercise **A**.

1. Kevin and I went to kindergarten together. We are _____ friends.
2. When I was a child, my father had a vegetable garden, so we ate lots of _____ fruit and vegetables.
3. I have to work long hours, and I'm always tired. I think I am _____.
4. My grandmother makes the best _____ chicken soup in the world! It's absolutely _____.

Conversation

A 🔊 5 Listen to the conversation. Choose the correct answer.

1. a. He started his new job.
   b. He doesn't like his new job.
   c. He doesn't want to get much exercise.
   d. He can't sleep and is always tired.

2. a. He should work less.
   b. He should find time to get more exercise.
   c. He should look for a more stress-free job.
   d. All the above.

B 🔊 5 Listen to the conversation again and fill in the blanks.

Doctor: Good morning, Mr. Lopez. How can I help you?

Mr. Lopez: Hello, doctor. _____, but when I go to bed _____.

Doctor: OK. How long have you had this problem?

Mr. Lopez: Since I started my new job.

Doctor: What do you do?

Mr. Lopez: I'm _____.

Doctor: How many hours do you work?

Mr. Lopez: I work about 80 hours a week.

Doctor: 80 hours! That's a lot. And how much exercise do you get?

Mr. Lopez: Not much. I don't have the time.

Doctor: OK. It seems to me that you are _____. You need to _____ and find time to _____. Maybe you should look for a more _____.

C Practice the conversation with a partner. Switch roles and practice it again.

D Change Mr. Lopez's problem to create a new conversation and practice it.

E | GOAL CHECK ✓ **Ask about lifestyles**

Ask a partner about his or her lifestyle.

D GOAL 4: Evaluate Your Lifestyle

When she's not watching sumo wrestling on TV, Yasu Itoman, 100, gets her own exercise by growing onions, tomatoes, carrots, and other herbs and vegetables in her garden. Her homegrown vegetables may help **prevent** cancer.

Listening

A Discuss the questions with a partner.

1. Do you want to live to be 100 years old?
2. What do you think you should do to live to be 100 years old?

B 🔊 6 Listen to the passage. Choose the correct answer.

1. If you have a healthy lifestyle, experts say you may live up to _____.
   a. 100 years old
   b. ten years longer
   c. 103 years old
   d. five years longer

2. How many times are there as many 100-year-old women as men in America?
   a. An equal number.
   b. Five times.
   c. Three times.
   d. Four times.

Word Focus

genes parts of the body that determine physical characteristics

joke to say something that is not serious

perfume liquid that smells good

prevent to avoid

run away to leave

Bosa, Sardinia

3. According to Willcox, what is the key to Okinawans' healthy lives?

   a. Reason for living.

   b. Wearing perfume.

   c. Regular exercise.

   d. Many more healthy nutrients.

4. What doesn't belong to a low-calorie diet?

   a. Miso soup.

   b. A small hamburger.

   c. A little fish.

   d. Okinawan vegetables.

C 🔊 **6** Listen to the passage again and answer the questions.

1. A long, healthy life mainly depends on two things. What are they?
   _____

2. Why do men live longer in Sardinia than in the United States?
   _____

3. How old was Ushi the last time the writer of the passage visited her?
   _____

4. What are the advantages of growing your own vegetables?
   _____

D GOAL 4: Evaluate Your Lifestyle

Communication

A Go around the class and find someone who does each of the following. Write the names in the chart, and then ask a follow-up question.

Find someone who . . .	Name
1. . . . plays a sport.	
2. . . . has a stress-free life.	
3. . . . has a clear reason for living.	
4. . . . has a grandparent more than 70 years old.	

Do you play a sport?

Yes, I do.

What sport do you play?

Min-jun plays football.

Seo-yeon has a stress-free life. She does yoga.

B Report to the class.

C Describe your own lifestyle. Answer the questions.

1. Do you lead a healthy lifestyle?
2. How often do you exercise?
3. What sort of food do you eat?
4. Do you get enough sleep?
5. How can you improve your lifestyle?

D GOAL CHECK ✓ **Evaluate your lifestyle**

Discuss with a partner the good habits and the bad habits in your lifestyles. Take turns. Give each other advice.

VIDEO JOURNAL: *The Science of Stress* E

Traffic can be very stressful.

Before You Watch

A Make a list of things that can cause stress. Discuss your list with a partner.

B Match the words with the definitions.

1. psychological _____
2. hormones _____
3. release _____
4. physical stress _____
5. mental stress _____
6. heart rate _____
7. soar _____
8. diabetes _____
9. neurological _____
10. bone density _____

a. stress on your body, like running
b. the rate at which the heart beats
c. the amount of bone mineral in bone tissue
d. concerned with a person's mind and thoughts
e. a medical condition in which someone has too much sugar in their blood
f. related to the nervous system
g. chemicals produced by your body
h. set free, liberate
i. rise rapidly
j. stress on your mind, like too much work

Word Focus

If you feel under **stress**, you feel worried and tense because of difficulties in your life.

Unit 2 Lifestyles 27

E VIDEO JOURNAL: *The Science of Stress*

While You Watch

A ▶ Watch the video. Circle **T** for *true* or **F** for *false*.

1. There are two types of stress: physical and mental.   T   F
2. Stress produces hormones.   T   F
3. When you exercise, you don't burn all the hormones.   T   F
4. Long-term hormones can cause problems.   T   F

B ▶ Watch the video again and choose the correct answer.

1. How can hormones help you manage the stress?
   a. Hormones make you feel happy.
   b. Hormones make you produce chemicals.
   c. Hormones rebuild our bodies.
   d. Hormones give you energy.

2. What does "kick in" mean in the sentence "Again those stress hormones are kicking in"?
   a. Begin to take effect. b. Pay for something.
   c. Hit violently with foot. d. Die.

3. Which problem is NOT caused by long-term stress according to the video?
   a. Heart disease. b. Diabetes.
   c. Obesity. d. Problems with bones.

4. Which of the following is NOT correct about the woman?
   a. Her body deals with physical stress pretty well.
   b. Her bone density is right on the norm.
   c. She doesn't need to care about mental stress.
   d. She shows no long-term effects from mental stress.

5. What does Kathy Matt and her team's research tell us?
   a. The effects of physical stress on the body are hard to measure.
   b. When we are under long-term mental stress, our bodies burn the extra fuel.
   c. We can not get to the end of the day with stress hormones.
   d. Not all stress is bad.

After You Watch

A Discuss the questions with a partner.

1. What did you learn from this video?
2. Will it change your lifestyle?

Communication

A Work in groups of three or four. You have been assigned to design your school's or office's Anti-Stress Campaign. Make a list of four things you will do.

FURTHER PRACTICE: *How Long Will You Live?*   F

Listening

A 🔊 7 Listen to the passage. What does the article say about these habits? Circle **good**, **bad**, or **no information** (the article doesn't say).

1. eating eggs and toast for breakfast every day   **good**   **bad**   **no information**
2. sleeping nine hours a night   **good**   **bad**   **no information**
3. going to the doctor every year   **good**   **bad**   **no information**
4. going for a walk after dinner every night   **good**   **bad**   **no information**
5. being very thin   **good**   **bad**   **no information**
6. drinking water every day   **good**   **bad**   **no information**
7. sunbathing for a short time every day   **good**   **bad**   **no information**
8. eating fruit for snacks every day   **good**   **bad**   **no information**

B 🔊 7 Listen to the passage again and answer the questions.

1. How many of the seven habits do you have? Which ones? _____
   _____
   _____

2. Which of the habits do you think is the easiest to do? Why? _____
   _____
   _____

3. Which of the habits do you think is the hardest to do? Why? _____
   _____
   _____

C 👥 Talk about a habit that you want to change. When did you start this habit? Why do you want to change it? How can you change it? Answer the questions and then report to the class.

Eric Whitacre Composer/Conductor
A VIRTUAL CHOIR 2,000 VOICES STRONG

Before You Watch

A Write the correct word under each picture.

| singer | conductor | choir | piano |

1. _____   2. _____

3. _____   4. _____

B Work with a partner. Try to think of one example each for items 1–4 in Exercise **A**. Share your answers with the class.

C Complete the sentences using the words from the box.

> **community** group of similar people
> **connection** relationship
> **post** put information up
> **record** store music so it can be listened to later
> **virtual** on a computer

1. The sisters had a very strong _____.

2. Please _____ your music for him.

3. People who live in a neighborhood are part of the _____.

4. The video game had a _____ world that players could play in.

5. I will _____ this information on the Web site for my classmates.

Eric Whitacre's idea worth spreading is that technology and music can connect us in wonderful, unexpected ways. Watch Whitacre's full TED Talk on TED.com.

D You are going to watch a TED Talk about a virtual choir. What do you think you will see in the video? What things do you think a person should do if they are going to start an online community? Discuss them with a partner.

> You should have a computer.

While You Watch

A Look at the pictures and quotes on the next page. Then watch the TED Talk. As you watch, put the pictures in order. Write the number in the box under the picture.

B Watch the TED Talk again. Complete the sentences using the words from the box.

| connect | singers | Malta |
| Sleep | Britlin | Jordan |

1. A girl named _____ posted a video for Eric Whitacre. Her video gave Eric the idea for the first virtual choir.

2. Eric created a virtual choir to _____ people around the world.

3. The second virtual choir had 2,051 _____.

4. The second virtual choir had singers from many countries, such as _____ and _____.

5. Eric Whitacre chose a piece called _____ for the second virtual choir.

"Human beings will go to any lengths necessary to find and connect with each other. It doesn't matter the technology."

— Eric Whitacre

"I had this idea: if I could get 50 people to all do this same thing, sing their parts—soprano, alto, tenor, and bass—wherever they were in the world, post their videos to YouTube, we could cut it all together and create a virtual choir."

"I just couldn't believe the poetry of all of it—these souls all on their own desert island, sending electronic messages in bottles to each other."

"For Virtual Choir 2.0 . . . our final tally was 2,051 videos from 58 different countries. From Malta, Madagascar, Thailand, Vietnam, Jordan, Egypt, Israel, as far north as Alaska, and as far south as New Zealand."

"I posted a conductor track of myself conducting. And it's in complete silence when I filmed it, because I was only hearing the music in my head, imagining the choir that would one day come to be."

TEDTALKS

Eric Whitacre Composer/Conductor
A VIRTUAL CHOIR 2,000 VOICES STRONG

Virtual Choir 2.0

After You Watch

A Read the sentences. Correct the false information.

1. A choir has to use the Internet. _____virtual choir_____

2. In Eric Whitacre's virtual choir, all the singers record their videos at the same time. _____

3. In their testimonials, the singers said that being in the virtual choir did not make them feel connected to other people around the world.
_____

4. All of the members of the choir are now good friends, even though they live in different countries and do not meet in person.
_____

B Most conductors work with singers in person, but Eric Whitacre conducts a choir online. With a group, take turns naming occupations. For each one, discuss whether it is possible for people in the occupation to work in a virtual way.

Teacher
- Teachers usually work in person.
- It is also possible for them to work in a virtual way. Teachers can teach online.

C Someone you know wants to be part of Eric Whitacre's next virtual choir. What advice would you give? With a partner, brainstorm a list of verbs (*be, learn, post,* etc.). Use *should/shouldn't* and the verbs to write five pieces of advice in your notebook.

Rural Alaska

D One woman in the virtual choir lives in rural Alaska, 400 miles from the nearest town. What do you think her life is like? Why is the choir important to her? How do music and technology connect her with people around the world? Discuss them with a partner.

E Do you like to do the following things online, in person, or both? Add your own idea. Then answer by placing a check (✓) in the appropriate box. Then interview your classmates about what they prefer. Write each classmate's initials in the appropriate box. Share with the class.

	Virtual world	In person	Both
1. play games			
2. take classes			
3. talk to family			
4. shop			
5. explore the world			
6. _____			

F Pick one of the activities in Exercise **E**. Write a short paragraph about why you think it is better to do that activity online or in person. Use some of the words provided.

| to live nearby/far away | to connect | to spend time together/alone |
| to feel lonely/alone | to meet | |

Challenge! What other virtual choirs has Eric Whitacre conducted? Visit TED.com to find out. Then share what you learned with a group. Be sure to include the name of the musical piece, the number of singers, the number of countries, and a short description of the piece. Use at least two descriptive adjectives.

UNIT 3 Achievements

A single climber stands on a peak above the clouds in Greenland.

Look at the photo, then answer the questions:

1. What has this person achieved?
2. What have you achieved in your life so far?

UNIT 3 GOALS

1. Talk about today's chores
2. Interview for a job
3. Talk about personal accomplishments
4. Discuss humanity's greatest achievements

A GOAL 1: Talk About Today's Chores

Vocabulary

A Label the pictures with phrases from the box.

- pay the bills
- buy the groceries
- sweep the floor
- cut the grass
- walk the dog
- vacuum
- iron the clothes
- put away the clothes

1. _____   2. _____   3. _____

4. _____   5. _____   6. _____

Word Focus

chore a task that must be done, but that many people find boring or unpleasant

7. _____   8. _____

B Which chores from Exercise **A** do you think are easy and which chores are difficult? Compare your opinions with a partner's.

C In your family, who does the household chores? Discuss it with a partner.

Conversation

A 🔊1 Listen to the conversation. Choose the correct answer.

1. a. Husband and wife.   b. Teacher and student.
   c. Mother and daughter. d. Employer and employee.
2. a. One.   b. Two.
   c. Three. d. Four.

B 🔊1 Listen to the conversation again and fill in the blanks.

Mom: Hi, honey. I'm home.

Lynn: Hi, Mom.

Mom: Have you _____?

Lynn: Yes, Mom. Of course I've _____. And I've _____.

Mom: And _____?

Lynn: Mom! I've been busy _____ and _____. I haven't had time.

Mom: Sorry, honey. It's just I've had a long day myself.

C Practice the conversation with a partner. Switch roles and practice it again.

D Replace the chores in the conversation in Exercise **B**, and practice the conversation again.

E GOAL CHECK ✓ **Talk about today's chores**

Talk to a partner about the chores you have done this week.

> **Real Language**
>
> We use *of course* to show something is obvious.

Unit 3 Achievements 37

B GOAL 2: Interview for a Job

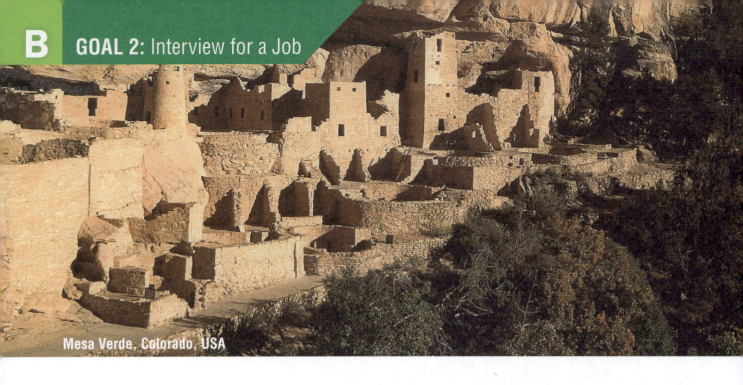

Mesa Verde, Colorado, USA

NEEDED URGENTLY!
TOUR GUIDE
Mesa Verde
Professional appearance. Good interpersonal skills. Experience an advantage. Driver's license essential. Call 2356 9845.

Miss Harmon

Mr. Reed

Listening

A 🔊2 Read the ad. Listen to Miss Harmon and Mr. Reed at the interview. Use the boxes on the left to take notes on their qualifications.

B 🔊2 The interviewers asked the following questions. Complete the questions. Listen again to check your answers.

1. Have you _____ from college?
2. Have you ever _____ as a tour guide?
3. Who is the most interesting person you have ever _____?
4. Have you _____ your driving test?

C 🔊2 Listen to the passage again and answer the questions.

1. Has Mr. Reed ever traveled abroad? _____
2. How many countries has Miss Harmon visited? _____
3. Who is the most interesting person Miss Harmon has met? _____
4. Has Mr. Reed passed his driving test? _____
5. Has Miss Harmon graduated from college? _____

D 🔄 Who should get the job? Discuss it with a partner.

Pronunciation: Reduced form of *have*

A 🔊 3 Listen to the examples. Notice the pronunciation of the reduced forms.

Full form	Reduced form
I have	I've
have you	/hæv-jə/
you have	you've
has he	/hæz-i/
she has	she's

B 🔊 4 Listen to the sentences. Check (✓) the correct column.

	Full form	Reduced form
1. **Has she** left?		
2. **Have you** finished?		
3. **Has he** read this book?		
4. **Have you** done your homework?		
5. **I have** never been to the USA.		

C 🔊 4 Listen again and repeat the sentences.

Communication

A Read the following ads. Then role-play an interview. For the first ad, **Student A** is the interviewer and **Student B** is the interviewee. Change roles for the second ad. When you are the interviewee, you can be yourself or pretend to be someone interested in the job.

WANTED!

Handyman for Kindergarten

Small kindergarten needs a person to help with maintenance—plumbing, carpentry, fixing our vehicles, etc. No experience with children necessary but must enjoy being around kids. Any age. $25 per hour.

LIFEGUARD

18–30 yrs old. You must be in very good shape. Must be able to swim 250 meters in 4 minutes and run 2,000 meters in 10 minutes. Experience an advantage. Some training offered.

Flexible hours.

B **GOAL CHECK** ✓ **Interview for a job**

Think of another job. What is required? Take notes. Interview a partner. Switch roles and repeat.

Unit 3 Achievements

C GOAL 3: Talk About Personal Accomplishments

Language Expansion: Personal accomplishments

A Label the pictures with phrases from the box.

1. _____ 2. _____ 3. _____

get a promotion
travel abroad
pass your driving test
run a marathon
get a credit card
graduate from high school/college

4. _____ 5. _____

6. _____

Word Focus

accomplishment
something remarkable that a person has done

B Check (✓) the achievements in Exercise **A** that you have done.

C Discuss with a partner about the things that he or she has achieved. What do you want to achieve this year/in college/in your life?

Conversation

A 🔊5 Listen to the conversation. Choose the correct answer.

1. a. Alfredo.   b. Pete.
   c. Both Alfredo and Pete.   d. Neither Alfredo nor Pete.

2. a. Two old friends are talking about their personal achievements.
   b. Two old friends are talking about how to open a new business.
   c. Two old friends are talking about where to buy a new house.
   d. Two old friends are making arrangements for their next meeting.

B 🔊5 Listen to the conversation again and fill in the blanks.

Alfredo: Hi, Pete. I haven't seen you for a long time. What's new?

Pete: Lots! I've quit my job _____, and I've _____.

Alfredo: Congratulations! When did you _____?

Pete: _____, and it's going well.

Alfredo: Great!

Pete: And what about you?

Alfredo: Things haven't changed much. I'm still _____. But I've _____. It's right next to Central Park.

Pete: Wow! Nice area.

Alfredo: Yeah. You should _____ some time.

Pete: Will do, when I have some time.

C Practice the conversation with a partner. Switch roles and practice it again.

D Change the words you filled in the blanks in Exercise **B** and practice the conversation again.

E GOAL CHECK ✓ Talk about personal accomplishments

Talk to a partner about your personal accomplishments or what you would like to achieve in the future.

Unit 3 Achievements 41

D GOAL 4: Discuss Humanity's Greatest Achievements

Listening

A What do you think are humanity's greatest achievements? Write your ideas in the following table.

Humanity's achievements	
1.	6.
2.	7.
3.	8.
4.	9.
5.	10.

B 🔊6 Listen to the passage. Circle **T** for *true* or **F** for *false*.

1. Humanity has lived on Earth for a long time.　　　　　　T　F
2. Many of humanity's greatest achievements are in science and technology.　　　　　　T　F
3. Antibiotics are machines.　　　　　　T　F
4. Art makes people happy.　　　　　　T　F
5. Humanity started to use fire a long time ago.　　　　　　T　F

C 🔊6 Listen to the passage again. Write down the achievements and examples mentioned.

Humanity's achievements	Examples of humanity's achievements
	_____, wheel
	_____, _____, _____, printing press
	_____, TV, computers, _____, _____
	music (_____ /Bach)
	_____ (the *Mona Lisa*)

D Answer the questions. Give your own opinions. Share your answers with a group.

1. Imagine life without electricity. How would it be different?
2. Many achievements have a negative effect. What are the negative effects of cars?
3. Do you think the *Mona Lisa* is a great achievement?
4. How would you define "great"?

Word Focus

antibiotic a medicine that kills bacteria. Penicillin is an antibiotic.

printing press a machine that prints books

The Louvre, Paris, France

HUMANITY'S GREATEST ACHIEVEMENTS

The Great Pyramids of Giza, Egypt

Unit 3 Achievements

D GOAL 4: Discuss Humanity's Greatest Achievements

An astronaut on the moon

▲ The *Mona Lisa*

Communication

A Here is a list of five important human achievements. Rank them in order of importance.

_____ the use of fire

_____ walking on the moon

_____ the Internet

_____ electricity

_____ antibiotics

_____ art

B Compare your list with a partner. Talk about your differences.

C | **GOAL CHECK** ✓ **Discuss humanity's greatest achievements**

Choose one important human achievement. It can be any achievement, not just from the listening. What do you know about it and why do you think it is important? Talk with a partner about the achievement you chose.

VIDEO JOURNAL: Spacewalk E

Before You Watch

A Match the words with the definitions.

1. spacewalk _____
2. radiation _____
3. minus _____
4. space shuttle _____
5. cosmonaut _____

a. (of temperature) below zero degree
b. a reusable spacecraft transporting people and cargo between Earth and space
c. an excursion by an astronaut or cosmonaut outside the spacecraft
d. a spaceman
e. powerful and dangerous rays sent out from radioactive substances

B Read the summary of the video and fill in the blanks with words from the box. Then watch the video and check your answers.

> weightless   survive
> underwater   oxygen
> solar panels

Video summary

In space, there is no _____. It is impossible to breathe. Sometimes astronauts have to make a spacewalk outside the spacecraft. In order to _____, astronauts wear special space suits. They do jobs like repair _____. It is dangerous work.

They prepare for their spacewalks _____ in special tanks. It is like being _____ in space but much safer.

Unit 3 Achievements 45

E VIDEO JOURNAL: *Spacewalk*

While You Watch

A Watch the video. Circle **T** for *true* or **F** for *false*.

1. It is always very cold in space.   T   F
2. Space suits are filled with oxygen.   T   F
3. The first person to walk in space was Edward White.   T   F
4. Astronauts fixed the solar panels on the Hubble Space Telescope.   T   F

B Watch the video again and choose the correct answer.

1. Which of the following is NOT mentioned as dangers in space?
    a. Lack of oxygen.
    b. The existence of radiation.
    c. The solar panels.
    d. Wild temperature fluctuations.

2. Soviet Cosmonaut, Alesksy Leonov "walked" in space for _____.
    a. 2 and half minutes
    b. 12 minutes
    c. 1 hour
    d. 10 hours

3. Astronauts take spacewalks in order to _____.
    a. discover whether man can survive in deep space
    b. maintain the International Space Station
    c. fix the Hubble Space Telescope
    d. all of the above

4. What measures do astronauts take to protect them against the dangers when they "walk" in space?
    a. They wear space suits.
    b. They work in pairs.
    c. They are connected to the spacecraft.
    d. All of the above.

5. Which of the following description of space suits is NOT correct?
    a. Space suits are made from a very strong material.
    b. Space suits make it possible for astronauts to survive in space.
    c. Space suits protect astronauts from weightlessness.
    d. Space suits make it difficult for astronauts to work in space.

After You Watch

A Scientific achievements can be expensive. The National Aeronautics and Space Administration (NASA) spent almost $18 billion in 2014. The Large Hadron Collider (a huge scientific instrument) cost $4.6 billion. Discuss these questions with a partner: Why do people spend a lot of money on big science projects? Is it worth it?

Communication

A China's aerospace achievements since its first manned space flight in 2003 are among the best in the world. What do you know about the Shenzhou spacecrafts? Do some research through the Internet and share your findings with a partner.

FURTHER PRACTICE: Amazing Achievements: Stephen Hawking   F

Listening

A 🔊7 Listen to the passage. Complete the following statements.

1. He has written _____.
2. Other scientists have called him _____.
3. He has _____ scientific papers.
4. He has won _____.
5. He has _____ in movies.
6. He has been _____.
7. He _____ around the world.
8. He has also traveled _____.

B 🔊7 Listen to the passage again and answer the questions.

1. What is Stephen Hawking's job?
   _____

2. What health problem does he have?
   _____

3. How does he get around?
   _____

4. How does he communicate?
   _____

5. What is he interested in now?
   _____

C What things have you done to improve your English? Talk about them with a partner or a group.

Unit 3 Achievements 47

UNIT 4
The Body

A man doing a back flip off of a tree stump in Mallorca Island, Spain

Look at the photo, then answer the questions:

1 What words could you use to describe the picture?

2 How does this kind of activity keep people healthy?

UNIT 4 GOALS

1. Discuss ways to stay healthy
2. Talk about lifestyles
3. Suggest helpful natural remedies
4. Explain cause and effect

A GOAL 1: Discuss Ways to Stay Healthy

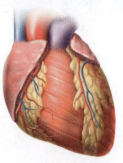

▲ human heart

▲ human fist

Vocabulary

A Look at the picture above. Then fill in the blanks with the words in the picture.

1. This pushes your blood through your body: _____
2. These carry blood around your body: _____, _____
3. These bring air into your body: _____
4. This covers the outside of your body: _____
5. This makes your body move: _____
6. This lets you think and remember: _____
7. This does many different things: _____liver_____
8. These digest food: _____, _____, _____
9. This supports your body: _____

☐ brain
☐ large intestine
☐ heart
☐ artery
☐ lungs
☐ vein
☐ stomach
☐ bone
☐ liver
☐ muscle
☐ small intestine
☐ skin

B 🔊 1 Listen and check (✓) the words you hear in the left box.

C List other parts of the body in the table.

shoulder				

Conversation

A 🔊 2 Listen to the conversation. Choose the correct answer.

1. a. Body parts.   b. Food and health.
   c. Lunch.   d. Keeping fit.
2. a. Brain.   b. Artery.
   c. Bone.   d. Lung.

B 🔊 2 Listen to the conversation again and fill in the blanks.

Ron: What are you eating? It looks better than my lunch.

Valerie: It's a fish stew, and it is good! Did you know that fish _____ _____ your brain?

Ron: Really? _____ anything else?

Valerie: Well, it's also _____, so it's probably good for your arteries.

Ron: And it's _____, right? So it could help you _____.

Valerie: Yes, I think you are right.

Ron: My lunch isn't _____ yours. I must have a cheese sandwich.

Valerie: But cheese has a lot of calcium. That's good for your bones.

Ron: That's right! Enjoy your lunch.

Valerie: You, too.

C 🔄 Practice the conversation with a partner. Then make a new conversation using foods you know about.

D 🔄 **GOAL CHECK** ✓ **Discuss ways to stay healthy**

Talk with your partner about things you do to stay healthy. Complete these sentences:

I try to _____.

I try not to _____.

I agree. Running is bad for your knees.

But it's harder work, so maybe it's better for your heart.

I try to get some exercise every day.

I try not to eat a lot of sugar.

Real Language

Common equative expressions include:

As soon as possible

As much as possible

Unit 4 The Body 51

B GOAL 2: Talk About Lifestyles

Word Focus

genes parts of a cell that control physical characteristics (eye color, height, etc.)

lifestyle how we live

Listening

A Discuss the questions with a partner.

1. What determines how healthy you are?
2. Are your genes or your lifestyle more important?

B 🔊 3 Listen to three people talking about their health. Match the speaker with the correct picture.

Speaker _____   Speaker _____   Speaker _____

C 🔊 3 Listen again and answer the questions.

1. What kind of exercise does Speaker A get?
   _____

2. Which family members does Speaker A mention?
   _____

3. What kind of exercise does Speaker B get?
   _____

4. How often does Speaker B get sick?
   _____

5. Why did Speaker C change her diet when she got older?
   _____

6. What do some people think about Speaker C's diet?
   _____

D Work with a partner. Interview each other. Then tell the class about your partner's lifestyle. Find out about:

- Exercise: What kind? How often?
- Diet: What do you usually eat?
- Genes: Do family members have health problems?
- Stress: How much and what kind?

Ask other questions about lifestyle that you think are important.

Pronunciation: Linking with comparatives and superlatives

> **Linking with comparatives and superlatives**
>
> When we use the comparative **-er** or **more**, and the next word starts with an /r/ sound, the words are linked together.
>
> When we use the superlative **-est** or **most**, and the next word starts with a /t/ sound, the words are linked together.
>
> *She'll run in a longer race next month.*   *We had the best time of our lives.*

A 🔊 4 Listen to the sentences. Notice how the sounds are linked. Listen again and repeat the sentences.

1. It's a stricter religion than my religion.
2. This is the best tea for your stomach.
3. My grandfather is a faster runner than I am.
4. Which exercise is the most tiring?
5. You'll need a better reason than that.

B Underline the sounds that link together. Then read the sentences aloud to a partner.

1. This is the longest text message I've ever seen.
2. Today's news was more reassuring than yesterday's news.
3. What's the best time of the day for you to study?
4. Flower experts are trying to develop a redder rose.
5. He took the softest towel in the house.

Engage!

Is your generation healthier or less healthy than your parents' generation?

Communication

A What are the best kinds of food and exercise for a healthy lifestyle? Rate the foods from least healthy (1) to healthiest (5). Add one idea of your own. Then do the same with the types of exercise. Compare your list with the list of another pair.

___ fruit   ___ bread   ___ meat   ___ vegetables   ___ _____

___ walking   ___ running   ___ swimming   ___ yoga   ___ _____

> I feel good if I eat some meat or fish every day.

> But is meat a healthier food than vegetables?

B **GOAL CHECK** ✓ **Talk about lifestyles**

Talk to a partner. Who are the healthiest people you know? What are some reasons for their good health?

Unit 4 The Body 53

C GOAL 3: Suggest Helpful Natural Remedies

Language Expansion: Everyday ailments

A Match the words with the definitions.

1. fever _____
2. sore throat _____
3. headache _____
4. hiccups _____
5. indigestion _____
6. pimple _____
7. nausea _____
8. insomnia _____

a. not being able to sleep
b. an uncomfortable feeling in the stomach because of something one has eaten
c. a small raised spot on the skin
d. a feeling like you are going to vomit
e. a feeling of pain in your throat
f. high body temperature
g. a repeated sound in your throat, often from eating too quickly
h. a pain in your head

B Read the article about natural remedies. What other natural remedies do you know about?

A Natural Solution

Garlic for a cold? Mint for bad breath? These days, more and more people are turning to their grandparents' remedies to cure their minor illnesses. And why not? These natural remedies are usually safe, inexpensive, and best of all—they work! (At least for some of the people, some of the time.) So the next time you're looking for a cure, skip the pharmacy and head to the grocery store for:

- **lemons** to stop the hiccups (Bite into a thick slice.)
- **ginger** to end nausea (Grind it and add hot water to make a tea.)
- **milk** to cure insomnia (Drink a warm glass at bedtime.)
- **honey** to help a sore throat (Mix it with warm water and drink it slowly.)
- **onions** to relieve a headache (Put slices on your forehead, close your eyes, and relax.)

garlic

lemon

If my skin feels dry, I put some olive oil on it.

olive oil

onion

ginger

54 新世界交互英语视听说 学生用书 2

Conversation

A 🔊 5 Listen to the conversation. Choose the correct answer.

1. a. She is thirsty.   b. She is hungry.
   c. She is tired.   d. She likes it.
2. a. To go for a walk. b. To go to bed.
   c. To drink coffee. d. To take the test.

B 🔊 5 Listen to the conversation again and fill in the blanks.

Olivia: Hi, Ashley. Are you drinking coffee? _____.

Ashley: Hi, Olivia. You're right. I usually don't drink coffee, but I need it today _____.

Olivia: You do _____. Did you get enough sleep last night?

Ashley: No, I _____ today's test, so it was hard _____.

Olivia: Come on. _____.

Ashley: _____? Why?

Olivia: To wake you up and _____ to your brain before the test.

Ashley: That's a good idea. Where do you want to go?

Real Language
We say *That's new* when we notice something different or unusual.

C Practice the conversation with a partner. Find and underline the three uses of the infinitive of purpose.

D Make a new conversation using your own ideas about health problems. Then role-play the conversation for the class.

E GOAL CHECK ✓ **Suggest helpful natural remedies**

Talk to a partner. What do you usually do to cure these common problems: a headache, bad breath, sore feet, and hiccups?

Unit 4 The Body

D GOAL 4: Explain Cause and Effect

Listening

A Talk to a partner. Which of these can make you sick?

- shaking hands with someone
- being outside in cold weather
- eating food
- riding a crowded bus
- touching your eye
- playing a computer game

B 🔊 6 Listen to the passage. Circle **T** for *true* or **F** for *false*.

1. Viruses can only live inside people or animals.   T F
2. All bacteria cause illnesses.   T F
3. Washing your skin can prevent some illnesses.   T F
4. Germs can enter the body through the eyes.   T F
5. After they kill germs, antibodies stay in the body.   T F
6. Vaccines kill germs in the body.   T F

Word Focus

sense see, hear, feel, etc.
influenza an illness cansed by a virus; the flu
cut opening in the skin
immune system the body's way of preventing illness
weak not strong

C 🔊 6 Listen to the passage again and match the causes with the effects.

Causes	Effects
1. viruses	a. sore throat and ear infection
2. bacteria	b. helping immune system to fight germs
3. immune system	c. illness
4. getting vaccinated	d. antibodies

For Your Information *Germs*

The English word *germ* is very common in everyday use, but it is not a scientific term. It refers to both bacteria and viruses, which are very different. One very common type of drug, antibiotics, is effective against bacteria but does not kill viruses. Because people don't understand the difference, they often want to take antibiotics for illnesses that won't be helped by them.

The immune system is the body's natural defense against illness.

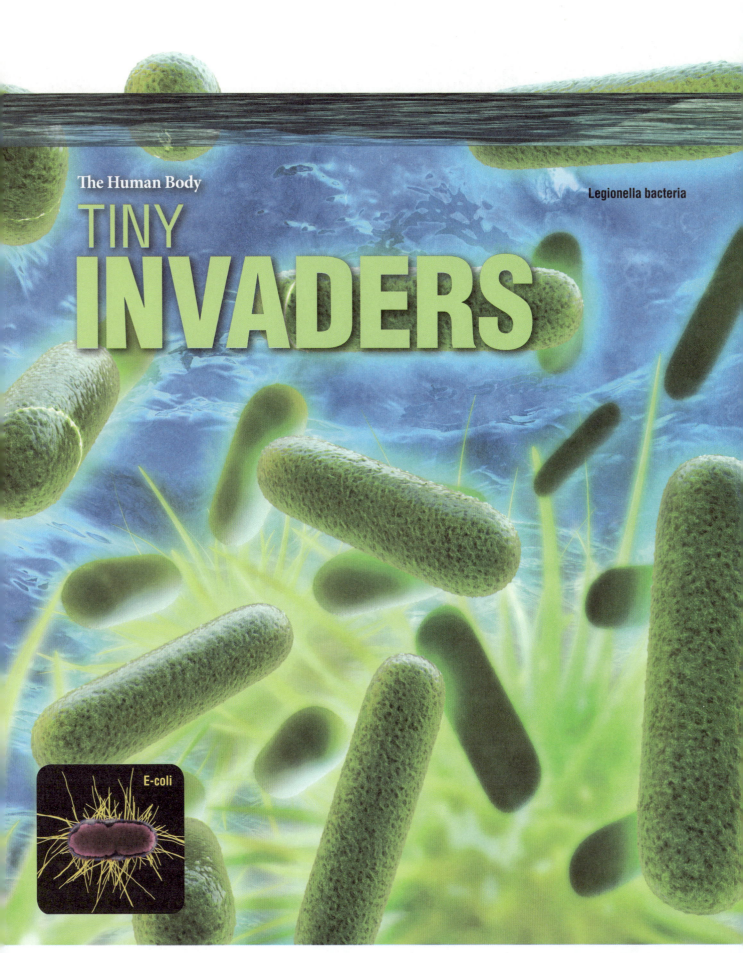

The Human Body
TINY INVADERS

Legionella bacteria

E-coli

D GOAL 4: Explain Cause and Effect

Communication

A Talk with your classmates. How does each action on the left spread illness? Which actions on the right prevent illness?

Ways to spread illness	Ways to prevent illness
Shaking hands	Staying home when you're sick
Coughing or sneezing	Washing your hands often
Drinking from a friend's water bottle	Covering your nose and mouth
Sitting near a sick person at school	Using clean dishes for eating and drinking
Eating food without washing your hands	Exercising and eating healthy food

B GOAL CHECK ✓ Explain cause and effect

Talk to a partner. What happens when viruses or bacteria enter the body?

> Shaking a person's hand can pass on bacteria.

> Staying home will help prevent spreading germs.

VIDEO JOURNAL: *The Human Body* E

Before You Watch

A Brainstorm five things your body lets you do every day.

B Write the meaning of the words with the help of a dictionary.

organ: _____

circulatory system: _____

respiratory system: _____

molecule: _____

digestive system: _____

esophagus: _____

enzyme: _____

intestine: _____

neuron: _____

reproductive system: _____

While You Watch

A Watch the video *The Human Body*. Draw lines to match the body's systems with the parts of the body or the cells they produce.

1. the circulatory system _____
2. the respiratory system _____
3. the digestive system _____
4. the nervous system _____
5. the reproductive system _____

a. the brain, spinal cord, and nerves
b. heart, veins and arteries
c. egg cells and sperm cells
d. the stomach and intestines
e. the lungs

B Watch the video again and circle **T** for *true* or **F** for *false*.

1. The heart is the body's strongest muscle.   T   F
2. Nutrients enter the blood from the small intestine.   T   F
3. The brain is about the size of an orange.   T   F
4. Another word for nerve cells is neurons.   T   F

Unit 4 The Body

E VIDEO JOURNAL: *The Human Body*

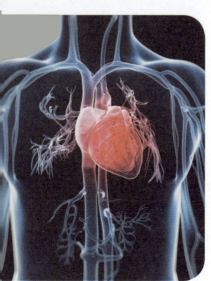

C ▶ Watch the video again and choose the correct answer.

1. How many cells are there in our body?
   - **a.** 100 million.
   - **b.** 100 trillion.
   - **c.** 100 billion.
   - **d.** 10 trillion.
2. How many times does the heart beat a day?
   - **a.** 100,000.
   - **b.** 1,000,000.
   - **c.** 10,000.
   - **d.** 10,000,000.
3. How long does the heart take to send blood on a complete trip around the body?
   - **a.** About two minutes.
   - **b.** More than one minute.
   - **c.** Within one minute.
   - **d.** Within two minutes.
4. Most nutrients enter the bloodstream through _____.
   - **a.** stomach
   - **b.** small intestine
   - **c.** large intestine
   - **d.** esophagus
5. Which one does not belong to the nervous system?
   - **a.** Brain.
   - **b.** Spinal cord.
   - **c.** Nerves.
   - **d.** Sperm.

After You Watch

A ♻ What information from the video surprised you the most? What are some things you can do to take care of your body's systems?

Communication

A ♻ Design a training program for an Olympic athlete. What will he or she eat every day? What kinds of exercise will they do, and how often? What else will help to get your athlete into top physical condition?

FURTHER PRACTICE: *In the Death Zone of Mount Qomolangma* F

Listening

A 🔊 7 Listen to the passage. Circle **T** for *true* or **F** for *false*.

1. The Death Zone is at the bottom of a mountain.   T   F
2. Health problems on high mountains come from not having enough oxygen.   T   F
3. Climbing Mount Qomolangma affects many parts of a climber's body.   T   F
4. On Mount Qomolangma, people breathe very slowly because the air is so thin.   T   F
5. Only a few people have climbed Mount Qomolangma.   T   F
6. New inventions have helped solve some health problems on Mount Qomolangma.   T   F
7. Climbers don't die on Mount Qomolangma nowadays.   T   F

B 🔊 7 Listen to the passage again. What happens to these parts of the body in the Death Zone? Match the columns.

1. heart ____
2. arteries ____
3. stomach ____
4. brain ____
5. skin ____
6. head ____

a. gets red
b. hurts a lot
c. works very slowly
d. carries blood faster
e. stops working
f. beats very quickly

C Answer the questions.

1. Why do you think people want to climb Mount Qomolangma?
2. What's the highest mountain in China? Would you like to climb it? Why or why not?

D 🗣 With a partner, talk about your favorite sport. What happens to people's bodies when they play it?

Unit 4 The Body

TEDTALKS

Lewis Pugh Adventurer/Environmentalist
MY MIND-SHIFTING QOMOLANGMA SWIM

Before You Watch

A Look at the pictures. Which of these places would you like to visit? Why? Research the places if needed. Tell a partner. Do you share the same answers?

Greenland

Patagonia

Mt. Qomolangma

Santa Cruz

Lewis Pugh's idea worth spreading is that we can do something to stop climate change; we just need to take it seriously. That's why he swam across Lake Imja, a place that should be made of ice. Watch Pugh's full TED Talk at TED.com.

TED Talk Summary

Lewis Pugh swims in cold places because it is _____ of saving the environment. He wants Earth to be _____, or around forever. Lewis decided to swim in a lake high on Mt. Qomolangma in the Himalayas. _____ helped him climb the big mountain to Lake Imja. After a failed first attempt, Lewis had a _____ to discuss the best way to swim at 5,300 meters (17,400 feet) above sea level. He is usually very _____ when he swims because he wants to finish quickly and get out of the cold water. But this time he showed _____ and swam slowly.

B Use the words in the box to complete the TED Talk summary.

| symbolic | humility | aggressive |
| Sherpas | debrief | sustainable |

WORD BANK
aggressive to do something with a lot of force
battleground a place where there are a lot of problems or conflict
debrief to talk about something after it is done
humility thinking you are not more important than other people or things
instability a situation that can change at any time
Sherpas people who live in the Himalayas and work as mountain guides
sustainable something that will last a long time
symbolic representing something
tactical something that is smartly planned

C Look closely at the pictures in Exercise **A** again. All of these places used to be completely covered in snow and ice. Discuss the following questions as a group.

What do you think is happening to the snow and ice in the pictures? Why? What do you think you will see in the TED Talk?

While You Watch

A Watch the TED Talk. Put the quotes in order. Write the number in the boxes provided.

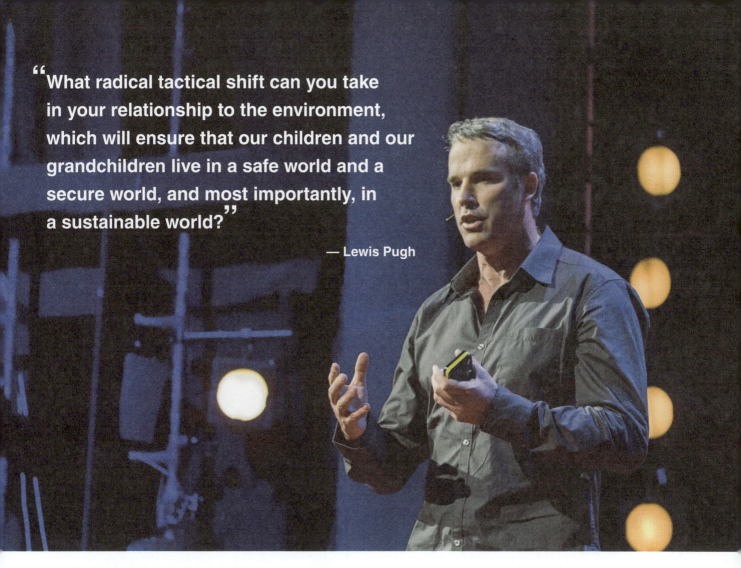

"What radical tactical shift can you take in your relationship to the environment, which will ensure that our children and our grandchildren live in a safe world and a secure world, and most importantly, in a sustainable world?"

— Lewis Pugh

"And I remember getting out of the water and my hands feeling so painful and looking down at my fingers, and my fingers were literally the size of sausages."

"I heard about this lake, Lake Imja. This lake has been formed in the last couple of years because of the melting of the glacier."

"And so I decided to walk up to Mt. Qomolangma, the highest mountain on this earth, and go and do a symbolic swim underneath the summit of Mt. Qomolangma."

"And I swam across the lake. And I can't begin to tell you how good I felt when I came to the other side."

Lewis Pugh Adventurer/Environmentalist
MY MIND-SHIFTING QOMOLANGMA SWIM

B ▶ Watch the TED Talk again. Circle the correct answer for each question.

1. What are the Himalayas? — big lakes — big mountains
2. How long did Lewis swim at the North Pole? — 19 minutes — 30 minutes
3. What is melting in the Himalayas? — glaciers — lakes
4. How many people depend on water from the Himalayas? — 2 billion — 1 million
5. What is the world's population? — 9 billion — 6.8 billion

After You Watch

A Fill in the names of the places from the words in the box.

| Lake Imja | North Pole | Bangladesh |
| Mt. Qomolangma | Himalayas | |

1. In 2007, Lewis Pugh swam at the _____ .
2. The glaciers in the _____ are melting.
3. The highest mountain on earth is _____ .
4. _____ is very high, near the top of Mt. Qomolangma.
5. China, India, Pakistan, and _____ are countries near the Himalayas.

B Use the emphatic adjectives to complete the sentences.

| exhausting | fascinating | enormous |
| excellent | awful | |

1. Mt. Qomolangma isn't small. It's a(n) _____ mountain.
2. His story wasn't boring. It was _____ .
3. Lewis Pugh survived his North Pole swim. He must be a(n) _____ swimmer.
4. Swimming for a very long time, especially in cold conditions, isn't easy. It is _____ .
5. When Lewis Pugh first tried the swim, he had to stop. He felt _____ .

64 新世界交互英语视听说 学生用书 2

A melting ice field

C Lewis Pugh completed his amazing swims to call attention to the problem of global warming. Here are some things caused by global warming. Write the correct captions under the pictures. Have you seen any of these things before? Give examples and discuss it with a partner.

Effects of Global Warming

| Animals in Danger | Huge Storms |
| No Water | Floods |

1. _____

2. _____

3. _____

4. _____

D Make a list of things you can do to protect the environment. Discuss it as a group. Share your list with other groups.

Challenge! Look at the pictures from Exercise **D** again. Research other effects of global warming. Make a list. Then research what China is doing to address the problem of global warming. Is it enough? Write an essay with your ideas to share with the class.

UNIT 5
Express Yourself

Crane workers on a construction site

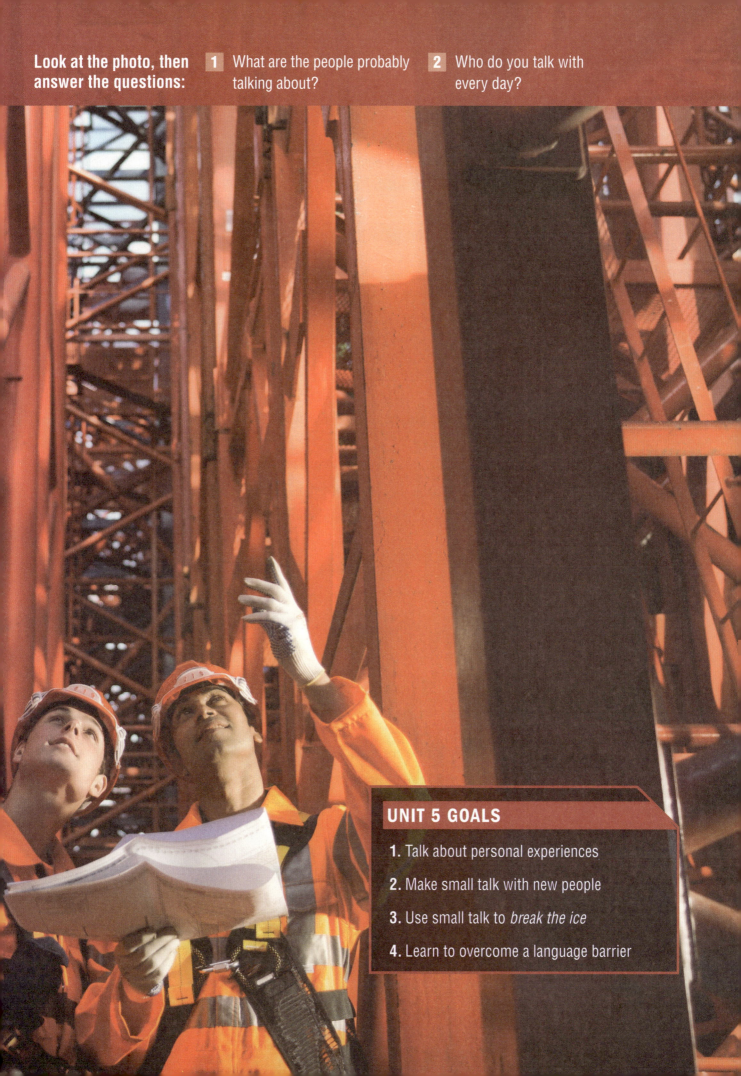

Look at the photo, then answer the questions:

1. What are the people probably talking about?
2. Who do you talk with every day?

UNIT 5 GOALS

1. Talk about personal experiences
2. Make small talk with new people
3. Use small talk to *break the ice*
4. Learn to overcome a language barrier

A GOAL 1: Talk About Personal Experiences

Vocabulary

A 🔊 1 Listen to the passage. Fill in the blanks.

Every culture around the world has different _____ and ways of communicating. When you learn a language, you learn more than words. You also learn a lot of rules. You learn what kind of greetings to use in different _____. For example, in English, we use formal and informal greetings. In China, a _____ greeting is "Have you eaten today?" In _____, there are rules for making _____ _____ when you meet a person. Once you have learned the rules of a language, you can communicate more easily and avoid _____.

People in different cultures also have different ways of using their bodies to communicate. We use our heads and hands to make _____, for example. But there's one kind of _____ that's the same everywhere. A _____ can always _____ people.

▲ A photographer talks with a Nepalese woman.

B Write the words you filled in the blanks of Exercise **A** next to the correct meanings.

1. _____ informal talk about everyday topics
2. _____ the act of expressing one's thoughts and feelings
3. _____ being part of the traditions of a country or people
4. _____ the act of adding something to something else
5. _____ usual ways of doing something
6. _____ movements used to communicate
7. _____ happy facial expression
8. _____ to join together
9. _____ what is happening at a particular time in a particular place
10. _____ problems caused when one is not understood

Word Focus

follow a rule do something the correct way
make small talk talk about things that aren't important

C 👥 Discuss the questions with a partner.

1. What are some problems you might face when talking with people from another culture?
2. What kinds of greetings do you know?
3. What gestures do you use when having a conversation with others?
4. Do you know any gestures used in other cultures? What do they mean?

Conversation

A 🔊 2 Listen to the conversation. Choose the correct answer.

1. a. To work in her company's office there.
   b. To learn Mexico's customs.
   c. To spend a month traveling there.
   d. To take Spanish lessons.

2. a. She is afraid of making mistakes.
   b. She has never been to Mexico before.
   c. She cannot speak any Spanish.
   d. She has never met people from Mexico.

B 🔊 2 Listen to the conversation again and fill in the blanks.

Annie: Guess what? I'm going to _____ in Mexico City.

Rick: That's great! What are you going to do there?

Annie: I'm going to _____ there. I'm a little _____, though. _____.

Rick: But _____ from Mexico, and you've _____ lessons.

Annie: That's true. And I guess I've learned something about Mexican _____.

Rick: It sounds to me like you're _____ to go.

Real Language

We use *Guess what?* in informal conversations to say that we have interesting news.

C Practice the conversation with a partner. Switch roles and practice it again. Tell your partner how you might feel about going to another country.

D GOAL CHECK ✓ **Talk about personal experiences**

Which of these things have you done or not done? Use the present perfect to tell a partner about your experiences.

- talk to someone from another culture
- communicate with gestures
- speak a foreign language
- make small talk with a stranger

▲ Palace of Bellas Artes, Mexico City

Unit 5 Express Yourself 69

B GOAL 2: Make Small Talk with New People

Listening

A 🔊 3 These people are meeting for the first time. Listen to their conversations. Where are the people?

Conversation 1 The speakers are in _____.

    a. a hospital   **b.** a school   **c.** an airport   **d.** a clinic

Conversation 2 These people are in _____.

    a. a restaurant   **b.** an apartment   **c.** an office building   **d.** a bank

B 🔊 3 Listen again. What do the people make small talk about?

Conversation 1 They make small talk about _____.

    a. classes   **b.** weather   **c.** clothes   **d.** music

Conversation 2 They make small talk about _____.

    a. sports   **b.** TV shows   **c.** the neighborhood   **d.** news events

C 🔁 Work with a partner. What will they talk about next? Think of two more ideas for each conversation.

For Your Information
Small talk

In many English-speaking cultures, people do not like to stand in silence for a long time with another person, even someone they don't know. It's considered polite to make small talk with strangers in situations that involve waiting together. It's also polite to make small talk at a party with other guests whom you don't know. Suitable topics for small talk are always general, not personal (such as sports, the weather, or upcoming holidays). They may also involve the situation that the two people are in—such as how they met the host at a party or how often they take the bus they are waiting for.

Pronunciation: *Have* or *has* vs. contractions

In statements with the present perfect tense, **have** and **has** are sometimes pronounced completely, but in informal speaking, contractions may be used.

A 🔊 4 Listen and repeat.

Have	Contraction	Has	Contraction
I have	I've	she has	she's
you have	you've	he has	he's
we have	we've	it has	it's
they have	they've		

B 🔊 5 Listen and circle the sentences you hear.

1. **a.** I have never gone skiing.   **b.** I've never gone skiing.
2. **a.** He has been to Colombia three times.   **b.** He's been to Colombia three times.
3. **a.** Linda has taken a scuba diving class.   **b.** Linda's taken a scuba diving class.
4. **a.** They have already eaten breakfast.   **b.** They've already eaten breakfast.
5. **a.** We have had three tests this week.   **b.** We've had three tests this week.
6. **a.** Michael has found a new job.   **b.** Michael's found a new job.

Communication

A Read the information.

> English-speakers often make small talk when they meet someone new. They have a conversation to get to know the other person. In general, small talk should make people feel more comfortable—not less comfortable—so the topics should not be very personal. For example, "Which department do you work in?" is a good question at work, but "How much money do you make?" is too personal.

B Circle the topics that are good for small talk when you meet someone for the first time. Then add two more ideas. Compare your ideas with a partner's.

school   money   family   work   sports   religion

_____   _____

C Read the situations. Circle the best question for each situation. Then practice conversations with a partner.

Situation 1 At work, Min-Hee talks to Judy. It's Judy's first day at her job.

    a. How old are you?   b. Are you new in this city?

Situation 2 Andrei is from Russia. He talks to Eduardo at the International Students' Club. It's Eduardo's first meeting.

    a. Where are you from?   b. Do you practice a religion?

Situation 3 Mark lives in apartment 104. He meets Lisa, his new neighbor.

    a. Which apartment do you live in?   b. Are you married?

D Which are good questions to ask when you meet someone new? Circle the letters.

a. Which classes are you taking now?
b. Who is your teacher?
c. What was your score on the placement test?
d. Have you studied at this school before?
e. When did you start working here?
f. How much did you pay for that car?
g. Have you lived here for a long time?
h. How much money do you earn here?

E **GOAL CHECK** ✓ **Make small talk with new people**

Pretend you are meeting your classroom partner for the first time (on the first day of class, waiting for the bus, or in another situation). Talk for two minutes.

C GOAL 3: Use Small Talk to *Break the Ice*

Language Expansion: Starting a conversation

A Read the questions in the box. Think of different ways to answer them.

Engage!

Are you shy or outgoing when you meet new people? Do you like to make small talk?

Starting a conversation
1. How do you like this weather?
2. Are you enjoying this class?
3. Did you hear about _____? (something in the news, for example)
4. How long have you been waiting? (for the elevator, the bus, the meeting to begin, etc.)
5. Have you always lived in this city?
6. Do you like living here?
7. What are you studying?
8. Who do you think will win the big game?
9. Which department do you work in?

B Choose one of the situations. Try to make small talk for as long as you can. Then change partners and practice again with another situation.

waiting in line in the office cafeteria   walking in the park
at a welcome party for new students   at the airport

▲ Cathedral in Bolivar Square in Bogota, Colombia

Conversation

A 🔊 6 Listen to the conversation. Choose the correct answer.

1. a. Impressive. b. Good. c. Boring. d. Interesting.
2. a. To ask Mr. Olsen how to do it. b. To call each other and talk about it.
   c. To finish it as soon as possible. d. To ask their classmates for the answer.

B 🔊 6 Listen to the conversation again and fill in the blanks.

Tom: Excuse me. Are you in my _____ class?

Rita: Yes! I saw you in class yesterday. I'm Rita.

Tom: Hi, Rita. I'm Tom. Is this your _____ class with Mr. Olsen?

Rita: Yes, it is, but I've heard _____ about him. What about you?

Tom: I've taken his classes before, and they've _____.

Rita: That's nice. Have you already done the homework for tomorrow?

Tom: No, not yet. What about you?

Rita: Not yet. Maybe we can _____ to _____ it.

Tom: That's a great idea! I'll give you my number.

> Have you ever taken a class with Ms. Lee before?
>
> Yes, I took an art class with her.

C Practice the conversation. Then practice the conversation with subjects you are studying and teachers from your school.

D GOAL CHECK ✓ Use small talk to *break the ice*

Move around the class. Walk up to five classmates and ask *icebreaker* questions.

Unit 5 Express Yourself 73

D GOAL 4: Learn to Overcome a Language Barrier

For Your Information
Annie Griffiths Belt

Annie Griffiths Belt studied photojournalism at the University of Minnesota in the United States and has worked for a number of magazines, including *LIFE*, *Geo*, *Smithsonian*, *Paris Match*, and *Stern*. She also spent a part of every year taking photographs for charity organizations such as Habitat for Humanity. She is a Fellow with the International League of Conservation Photographers, and her book *Last Stand: America's Virgin Lands* raised $250,000 for conservation projects. She has written a memoir about her work called *A Camera, Two Kids and a Camel*. She lives in the United States with her husband, Don, and two children, Lily and Charlie.

Word Focus

landscapes broad view of the land

overwhelmed very emotional

rewarding a valuable experience

Listening

A Discuss these questions with a partner.
1. Have you ever taken a picture of people you didn't know? How did you do it?
2. What kinds of photographs do you like? What makes those photographs good?
3. What are the advantages and disadvantages of being a photographer?

B 🔊 7 Listen to the passage. Circle **T** for *true* or **F** for *false*. Then correct the false sentences.

1. Griffiths has never traveled to England. T F
2. Griffiths has never traveled to Antarctica. T F
3. Petra is a very old city in Jordan. T F
4. Griffiths can only connect with English-speakers. T F
5. Most people do not want Griffiths to take their picture. T F
6. Volunteering is one way to begin a photography career. T F

C 🔊 7 Listen to the passage again and choose the correct answer.

1. a. 1970.   b. 1978.   c. 1917.   d. 1980.
2. a. Continents.   b. Green landscapes.
   c. Ancient cities.   d. Different cultures and regions of the world.
3. a. Knowing how to break the ice.   b. Traveling around the world.
   c. Using a high-end camera.   d. Making friends with new people.
4. a. Greetings.   b. Small talk.   c. A smile.   d. Shaking hands.

Communication

A Which actions can help people from different cultures to communicate? Which actions are not helpful for communication? Talk with a partner.

- smile at people you don't know
- use gestures to communicate
- say nothing if you don't know the right word
- pretend to understand everything
- ask people about words in their language
- other _____

TAKING PICTURES OF THE WORLD

Portrait by Annie Griffiths

B Talk to your classmates about some places you have traveled to. How did you communicate with the people in those places? Then make a list of Dos and Don'ts for communicating with people who speak a different language. Write them in the boxes in the chart below.

Dos	Don'ts
1.	1.
2.	2.
3.	3.
4.	4.
…	…

C Compare your answers with a partner's.

D GOAL CHECK ✓ **Learn to overcome a language barrier**

In what professions do people need to overcome language barriers quickly in order to do their jobs? Talk with a partner about different ways they can do this.

> Do smile at people.

> Don't expect them to know your language.

Unit 5 Express Yourself 75

E VIDEO JOURNAL: *Orangutan Language*

▲ Ancient acacia trees near the red sand dunes of the Namib Desert

For Your Information
Orangutans

Orangutans are the largest tree-dwelling animals in the world. They are currently found in the rainforests of Borneo and Sumatra. The males are about 145 centimeters (4 feet, 9 inches) in height and weigh over 118 kilograms (260 pounds), and females are around 127 centimeters (4 feet, 2 inches) in height and weigh around 45 kilograms (100 pounds). Their usual diet is fruit, but they also eat insects, honey, and bird eggs. They are very intelligent. They use tools to get fruit, and scientists have seen orangutans using leaves to make rain hats!

Before You Watch

A Read the following sentences. Choose the one that is closest in meaning to the underlined word.

1. A growing number of people have started to show great concern over wildlife conservation.
   a. prevention   b. promotion   c. protection   d. presentation

2. The computer is not responding quickly enough, but the orangutan is doing the exercises correctly.
   a. reacting   b. calculating   c. functioning   d. connecting

3. It is incredibly important for a person to have an aim in life.
   a. basically   b. certainly   c. actually   d. extremely

4. She was wearing a rose to help him to identify her.
   a. introduce   b. recommend   c. recognize   d. guide

5. Dinosaurs have been extinct for millions of years.
   a. distinct   b. distinctive   c. nonexistent   d. instinctive

B Read the summary of the video and fill in the blanks with the words from the box. Then watch the video and check your answers.

> stimulating   exhibit   symbols   voluntary   primates

At the National Zoo in Washington D. C., Rob Shumaker runs the Orangutan Language Project. Orangutans are large, intelligent _____. They aren't able to speak like humans, but they can learn to connect _____ to real objects. Shumaker believes the language program is mentally _____ for the orangutans. The program is _____ so the animals can choose to participate or not. It's part of a zoo _____ called "Think Tank" which explores the process of thinking.

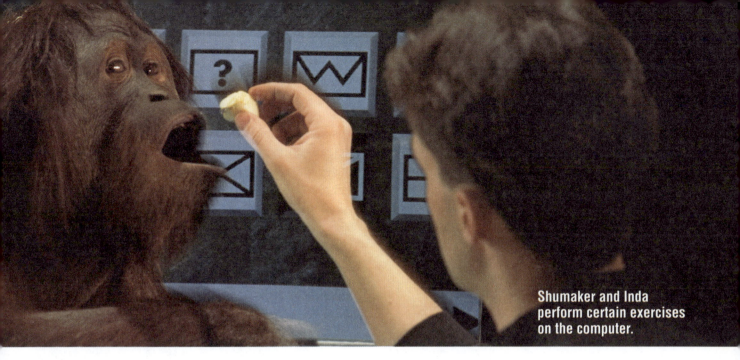

Shumaker and Inda perform certain exercises on the computer.

While You Watch

A ▶ Watch the video. Circle **T** for *true* or **F** for *false*.

1. In Malay, the word orangutan means "person of the jungle". T F
2. The orangutans in the video are Inda and Azie. T F
3. The orangutans work with symbols on paper. T F
4. The orangutans are brother and sister. T F
5. Wild orangutans could become extinct in 8 to 10 years. T F

B ▶ Watch the video again and choose the correct answer.

1. Where do orangutans come from?
   a. Indonesia and Malaysia.
   b. Australia and New Zealand.
   c. USA and Canada.
   d. Guinea and Uganda.
2. What choices does the zoo give the orangutans?
   a. Where to go.   b. What to do.   c. What to eat.   d. Both a and b.
3. How old is Inda, the female orangutan?
   a. 10.   b. 20.   c. 12.   d. 22.
4. How does Inda get her point across?
   a. By using gestures.
   b. By speaking.
   c. By using symbols.
   d. By drawing.
5. What do zoo officials hope exhibits like Think Tank will do?
   a. Entertain the visitors with more orangutans.
   b. Teach the orangutans to play more games.
   c. Train the orangutans to speak like humans.
   d. Educate the public and increase conservation efforts.

E VIDEO JOURNAL: *Orangutan Language*

After You Watch

A Brainstorm several ways in which animals communicate. Compare animal communication with human communication. Then make a list of their similarities and differences. Individually write them in the boxes in the chart below. Compare your answers with a partner's.

Similarities	Differences
1.	1.
2.	2.
3.	3.
4.	4.
…	…

Communication

A You have the opportunity to create a new way to write English. Think of ten English words that are difficult to spell. Make a word list with a better way to write the words. Share your word list with the class to see whether your classmates can guess all the words.

Words difficult to spell	A better way to write the words
1.	1.
2.	2.
3.	3.
4.	4.
5.	5.
6.	6.
7.	7.
8.	8.
9.	9.
10.	10.

FURTHER PRACTICE: Drinking Tea, Breaking the Ice   F

Listening

A 🔊 8 Listen to the passage. Circle **T** for *true* or **F** for *false*.

1. In 1993, Mortenson wanted to climb a mountain in Pakistan called K2.   T   F
2. In *Three Cups of Tea*, Mortenson talks about his experiences climbing K2.   T   F
3. Mortenson stayed on the mountain for 70 days, but failed to reach the top.   T   F
4. Mortenson has built 17 schools in Pakistan and Afghanistan.   T   F
5. Mortenson found a good way to break the ice: by smiling at people.   T   F

B 🔊 8 Listen to the passage again and match the sentence beginning with the correct reason.

1. Mortenson wanted to build a school ___
2. Mortenson tried to get money ___
3. Some people didn't like him ___
4. Mortenson's work wasn't easy ___
5. Mortenson drank tea with people ___

a. because he wanted to connect with them.
b. because the people in Korphe helped him.
c. because he wanted to build a school.
d. because he built schools for girls.
e. because he was from another country.

C 🗣 With a partner, talk about a time when you met a new person. Where did you meet this person? How did you break the ice?

Unit 5 Express Yourself   79

UNIT 6

Cities

Japanese-inspired "Shibuya" style crossing at Oxford Circus in London

Look at the photo, then answer the questions:

1 What can you find in a city?

2 What is your city famous for?

UNIT 6 GOALS

1. Describe your city or town
2. Explain what makes a good neighborhood
3. Discuss an action plan
4. Make predictions about cities in the future

A GOAL 1: Describe Your City or Town

▲ Shibuya Crossing outside Shibuya Station in Tokyo, Japan

Vocabulary

A 🔊 1 Listen to the passage. Fill in the blanks.

People hold different views on _____ life. Some people claim that it is great. There is good _____ _____, like trains and buses. And we also have _____ where cars can go fast. People can find good jobs. And after work, there is great _____ in restaurants and dance clubs. Cities get bigger every year because they are the best places to live. But others argue that city life is terrible. Cities are so _____, with too many people in a small area, and the _____ grows every year. There is too much _____, because people want to drive everywhere. It's always noisy. A lot of people want to live in a _____ area, but there aren't many jobs. It's better to live in a _____ and _____ to a job by car. Which one do you agree with?

B Write the words you filled in the blanks of Exercise **A** next to the correct meanings.

1. _____ in the city
2. _____ roads where cars go fast
3. _____ travel to your job
4. _____ trains, buses, and subways
5. _____ number of people
6. _____ things to do in the evening
7. _____ cars moving on a street
8. _____ too full
9. _____ outside the center of a city
10. _____ in the country

C Work with a group. Discuss what kind of life you prefer: city life, suburban life or country life? Support your opinions with facts. Share and compare your ideas with the class.

Word Focus

traffic jam so many cars in the street that they can't move

population growth more people living in a place

▲ Bongeunsa Temple in Seoul, South Korea

Conversation

A 🔊 2 Listen to the conversation. Choose the correct answer.

1. a. New York. b. Seoul. c. New Zealand. d. Singapore.
2. a. Positive. b. Negative. c. Indifferent. d. Critical.

B 🔊 2 Listen to the conversation again and fill in the blanks.

Mark: So, _____, Mimi?
Mimi: I _____ New York now, but I _____ in Seoul.
Mark: Really? I've never been to Seoul. _____?
Mimi: Well, some people think it's _____, but it has _____.
Mark: I've heard that it's _____.
Mimi: That's true, but it's _____ now. In the future, it will be _____.

C 🔄 Practice the conversation with a partner. Switch roles and practice it again.

D Check (✓) the things that are true about your city. Add some ideas of your own.

Bad things about your city		Good things about your city	
It's ____.		It has great ____.	
☐ noisy	☐ boring	☐ restaurants	☐ beaches
☐ dangerous	☐ crowded	☐ parks	☐ museums
☐ expensive	☐ polluted	☐ neighborhoods	☐ nightlife
_____	_____	_____	_____

E 🔄 **GOAL CHECK** ✓ **Describe your city or town**

With a partner, make a new conversation about your city. Then make new conversations about two other cities you know.

Unit 6 Cities 83

B GOAL 2: Explain What Makes a Good Neighborhood

Listening

▲ The Jardin Nomade in Paris

A Discuss these questions with a partner.
1. How often do you go to a park?
2. What do you do there?
3. What do you think about the parks in your city or town?

B 🔊 3 Listen to a radio program about a park in Paris called the Jardin Nomade. Choose the correct answer.

1. The Jardin Nomade is in _____ area.
   a. a rural   b. an urban   c. a suburban   d. a hilly
2. The Jardin Nomade is amazing because it's so _____.
   a. big   b. small   c. old   d. modern
3. In the Jardin Nomade, people _____.
   a. grow food   b. go swimming   c. enjoy art   d. sun themselves

C 🔊 3 Listen again and answer the questions.
1. What year did the park start? _____
2. How many gardens do people have in the park? _____
3. What do the neighbors eat there every month? _____
4. How many people come to the monthly dinners? _____
5. How many parks like this are there in Paris now? _____

Pronunciation: Emphatic stress

A 🔊 4 Listen and repeat the exchanges. Notice how the underlined words sound stronger.
1. **A:** Is your city <u>expensive</u>?
   B: Yes, it's <u>really</u> expensive!
2. **A:** Do you like living in an <u>apartment</u>?
   B: No, I like living in a <u>house</u> much more.
3. **A:** Is your neighborhood <u>new</u> or <u>old</u>?
   B: The houses are very <u>old</u>.
4. **A:** Can you <u>walk</u> to school?
   B: No, I <u>can't</u>. It's too <u>far</u>.

B Read the exchanges in Exercise **A** with a partner. Stress the underlined words.

C Take turns asking and answering three questions about your neighborhood. Stress the important words.

Engage!
What are some new things in your city?

For Your Information
Urban gardens

Around the world, a surprising amount of food is grown on small plots of land in urban environments. An estimated 800 million people are now involved in urban agriculture in different cities. In Mumbai, India, an urban farm was created at a school to give employment to street children and provide healthy food for slum residents. In Seattle, USA, the P-Patch program has land in 70 different neighborhoods where people can have their own gardens for a small fee.

Are there any <u>parks</u> in your neighborhood?

Yes, there are <u>two</u>.

Conversation

A 🔊 5 Listen to the conversation. Choose the correct answer.

1. a. It looks very old because there are a lot of old buildings.
   b. There is no supermarket at all in her neighborhood.
   c. Its only supermarket makes food very expensive.
   d. Its supermarket can't provide people in the neighborhood with adequate food.
2. a. High food prices force people in this neighborhood to shop online.
   b. A large variety of stores are needed in this neighborhood.
   c. The problem in the woman's neighborhood can't be solved.
   d. People have to move from the neighborhood owing to the lack of stores.

B 🔊 5 Listen to the conversation again and fill in the blanks.

Ben: _____ living in your neighborhood?

Sarah: Well, it has a lot of _____, but there are _____.

Ben: Like what?

Sarah: It doesn't have _____. There's _____, so _____.

Ben: That sounds like a pretty _____.

Sarah: It is, but the city is building a new _____ now. Next year, we'll have _____.

C Practice the conversation with a partner. Switch roles and practice it again.

D Write the words or phrases from the box in the correct column. Add two more ideas to each column. Make two new conversations using these ideas.

Good things in a neighborhood	Bad things in a neighborhood

> beautiful buildings
> crime
> a lot of noise
> heavy traffic
> public transportation
> pollution
> trees and green space
> many different stores

E What are the three most important things for a good neighborhood? Talk about your ideas in Exercise **D**. Make a new list with a group. Give reasons.

Most important things for a good neighborhood	Reason
1.	
2.	
3.	

F GOAL CHECK ✓ **Explain what makes a good neighborhood**

Explain your group's list to the class.

Unit 6 Cities 85

C GOAL 3: Discuss an Action Plan

Language Expansion: Using maps

A Study the map. Write the word from the box in the correct space.

South   symbols   East   key   West   scale

B Take turns asking and answering the questions.

Where's the train station?

It's in the north of the city.

1. In which parts of the city are the libraries?
2. Where are the public sports centers?
3. Where will the new road be?
4. How many shopping centers does the city have now? How many do you think it will have in 2020?
5. What do you think this city needs?

Conversation

A 🔊 6 Listen to the conversation. Choose the correct answer.

1. a. How to have a neighborhood meeting.
   b. How to get a library in their neighborhood.
   c. How to get the books in the neighborhood library.
   d. How to write a letter to the newspaper.

2. a. It is very uncommon to have a library in the neighborhood.
   b. There are various meetings in the neighborhood to be held.
   c. Whether the library should be built or not is decided by the newspaper.
   d. Public opinions should be taken into consideration in building a library.

B 🔊 6 Listen to the conversation again and fill in the blanks.

Jennie: This neighborhood really _____.

Dan: You're _____. But how can we _____?

Jennie: I think we should have a _____ to talk about it.

Dan: That's a good idea. And after we have the _____, we'll _____.

Jennie: Great! I'll help you.

C Make new conversations with a partner to talk about places in your neighborhood.

D GOAL CHECK ✓ **Discuss an action plan**

What does your city need? List things you can do to make your plan happen. Use time clauses to discuss when you will do each thing on the list. Then compare your list with a partner's.

D GOAL 4: Make Predictions About Cities in the Future

Listening

A How did people get their food in the past, and what kinds of food did they eat? How is it different from our food today? How will it change in the future? Use the words below. Share your ideas with a partner.

| produce | healthy food | grow | distribute | transport |

B 🔊 7 Listen to the passage. Circle **T** for *true* or **F** for *false*.

1. Cities need safe and healthy food.   T   F
2. If we know how people in the past got food in cities, we can do the same things that they did.   T   F
3. It takes a lot of fossil fuel to produce food.   T   F
4. Compared with ancient food routes, our ways of producing food are more efficient.   T   F
5. In the future, we will need to change the way we grow food.   T   F

C 🔊 7 Listen to the passage again and choose the correct answer.

1. a. Everyone will naturally associate it with agriculture.
   b. We all know who grew our food and who harvested it.
   c. We assume it can be easily found in any restaurant or supermarket.
   d. We definitely know how it got from the farm to the city.
2. a. How ancient food routes shaped our modern cities.
   b. How our ancestors grew and distributed food.
   c. How people can reduce the use of fossil fuel in modern cities.
   d. How people change their dietary habits.
3. a. Twice as many people will live in the suburbs as do now.
   b. It will be very difficult to feed ourselves.
   c. Fossil fuels will be replaced by renewable energy.
   d. We will consume twice as much meat and dairy as we do today.
4. a. It is heavy in meat and dairy.
   b. It is heavy in processed food.
   c. It excludes products from animal resources.
   d. It requires enormous amounts of energy to produce.
5. a. Reducing ingestion of fried and high fat foods.
   b. Growing our own food at home.
   c. Eating more fruits and vegetables.
   d. Producing food closer to our cities.

For Your Information
Carolyn Steel

Carolyn Steel is an architect, a food urbanist, and the author of the book *Hungry City*. Born and raised in central London, Steel says she has always had a fascination with buildings and how they are inhabited. She was interested not only with the architecture of the buildings, but also in the relationship between the buildings and what happens within them. This interest in how things are connected led her to focus on food and architecture and the importance of food in the development of cities worldwide. Steel wants to make us aware of how the growth of cities in the past was connected to the food the inhabitants ate, and how this connection has been lost in modern cities. This loss, she argues, has a negative effect on the planet and our lives. She strongly believes that we need to re-evaluate how we grow and produce food, how far it is transported, and our relationship with nature.

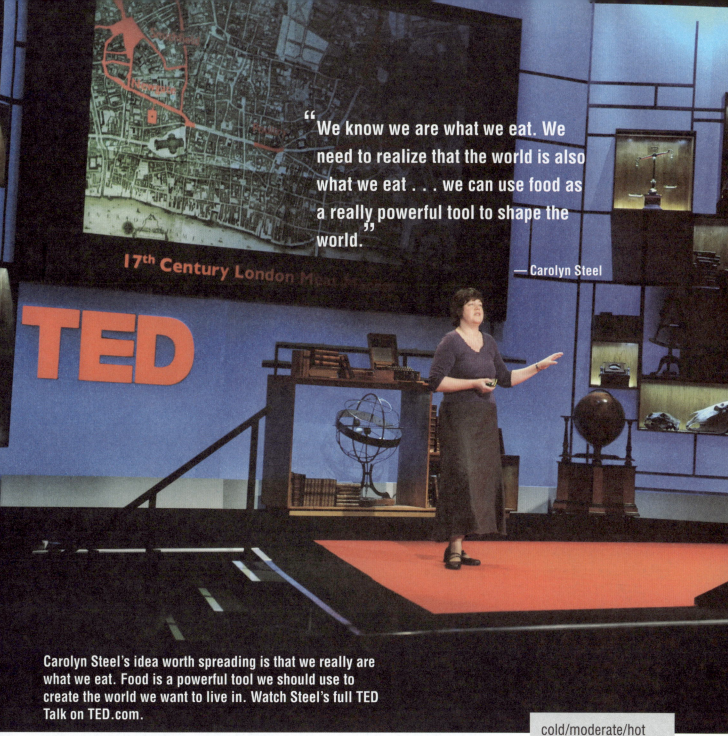

"We know we are what we eat. We need to realize that the world is also what we eat . . . we can use food as a really powerful tool to shape the world."

—Carolyn Steel

Carolyn Steel's idea worth spreading is that we really are what we eat. Food is a powerful tool we should use to create the world we want to live in. Watch Steel's full TED Talk on TED.com.

Communication

A Share your ideas of how food has shaped your city with a partner. Think about your city's location, its environment, and its culture. Use the words in the box.

cold/moderate/hot
climate   ocean
inland   hunting
fishing   immigrants
native people

B **GOAL CHECK** ✓ **Make predictions about cities in the future**

Work with a group. Predict the cities in the future. Use the words in the box to make your prediction. Share your opinions and support them with facts. Which predictions are the most/least realistic?

population   climate
transport   resources
traditions   environment
eating habit

Unit 6 Cities 89

E VIDEO JOURNAL: Fes

Before You Watch

A Match the words with the definitions.

1. masterpiece _____
2. restore _____
3. fountain _____
4. preserve _____
5. heritage _____
6. testament _____
7. refugee _____
8. poverty _____
9. antiquity _____
10. woe _____

a. thing that provides clear proof of something
b. great sorrow or distress
c. object that dates from ancient times
d. state of being poor
e. excellent art
f. put into good condition again
g. water pushed into the air in a beautiful way
h. keep in good condition
i. beliefs and traditions that came from the past
j. a person who has been forced to leave his country or home, often due to political or religious persecution

For Your Information
Fes

- Fes is the third largest city in Morocco, with a population of one million in 2010.
- The name of the city is sometimes spelled *Fez*.
- It's one of Morocco's "Four Imperial Cities" (with Marrakech, Meknes, and Rabat).
- Al-Karaouine University in Fes is the oldest continuously operating university in the world.
- The medina (old city) in Fes is believed to be the largest car-free urban area in the world.
- Popular tourist sites in Fes include the Bouananiya Medersa (in the video) and the Bab Bou Jeloud gate. Visitors can shop for brassware, leather, pottery, and other traditional crafts.
- The traditional Middle Eastern hat called the *fez* actually comes from Greece—not Fes!

B Fill in the blanks. Use the phrases in the box.

| at least | a new lease on life | step in | take second place to |
| take a toll | in practice | in theory | |

1. Since recovering from her operation, she's had _____.
2. An occasional indulgence is fine, but too much dessert can _____ on waist lines.
3. My personal life has had to _____ my career.
4. It can be a dangerous course of action which might be sound _____ but perhaps a trifle risky _____.
5. If no agreement was reached, the army would _____.
6. _____ this meeting had helped to thaw the atmosphere.

While You Watch

A Watch the video. Circle **T** for *true* or **F** for *false*.

1. The city of Fes was founded in the ninth century. T F
2. By the 1300s, Fes was a center for science and learning. T F
3. The government isn't interested in restoring the historic buildings in Fes. T F
4. In the future, the Medersa will be a museum. T F
5. Restoration is not the only solution to the preservation of the city's architectural heritage. T F

B Watch the video again and choose the correct answer.

1. What are the restorers doing in the Bouananiya Medersa?
   a. Taking old paint off the walls of the Medersa.
   b. Carving on the walls of the Medersa.
   c. Cleaning the graffiti off the wall of the Medersa.
   d. Whitewashing the carvings on the wall.
2. How important is medina in Fes today?
   a. It is one of the cultural capitals of Islamic heritage.
   b. It is the political, economic and cultural center.
   c. It is a living museum of Morocco's Islamic heritage.
   d. It is the best-preserved Islamic medina in the Arab world.
3. Why is historic preservation of medina not given priority?
   a. Because it is unnecessary to preserve the historic homes that aren't falling down.
   b. Because poverty makes people in medina have more basic concerns.
   c. Because the government can't raise enough funds to support it.
   d. Because there is no organization responsible for it.
4. Who is protecting Fes's historic buildings in practice?
   a. Private citizens.
   b. Private foundations.
   c. Professional institutions.
   d. The government and institutes.
5. What is the ultimate source of Fes's woes?
   a. Property.
   b. Poverty.
   c. Historic homes.
   d. Architectural heritage.

> The Bouananiya Medersa in Fes, Morocco, is a **masterpiece** of art. It's in very bad condition now, but people are working to **restore** its walls and **fountains**. Some old buildings in Fes are in danger because **wealthy** people buy and take away pieces of them. Now, **private** organizations are trying to **preserve** these buildings for the future. They hope all people can enjoy Morocco's **heritage**.

E   VIDEO JOURNAL: *Fes*

▲ Bouananiya Medersa in Fes, Morocco

After You Watch

A What are some important buildings and places in your city's heritage? Make a list and then share the information with a partner.

Communication

A Suppose some foreign visitors come to a historic place in your city and ask you to be a guide. How will you answer their questions:

1. What happened there?
2. What can visitors see and do there?
3. How much does it cost to visit?
4. What hours is it open?
5. How can visitors get there?

FURTHER PRACTICE: *Forests for Cities* F

Listening

A 🔊 8 Listen to the passage. Circle **T** for *true* or **F** for *false*.

1. Kasugayama Forest lies in a rural area of Nara, Japan. **T F**
2. With a history of more than 1,000 years, Kasugayama Forest is the oldest urban forest in the world. **T F**
3. All urban forests which have many good effects on the environment are parks. **T F**
4. There are many more trees in Thames Chase than in Kasugayama Forest. **T F**
5. Thames Chase in London is a great location for walking and cycling. **T F**
6. Without space for a big urban forest, some old cities are unlikely to have more green space. **T F**
7. According to the passage, people spend more time at shopping centers that have trees. **T F**
8. Urban forests will play a positive role in people's life in the future. **T F**

B 🔊 8 Listen to the passage again. Write about the good effects of urban forests.

Good effects on the environment
1. Take
2.
3.   because
a.
b.
Good effects on people
4.
5.
6.

C 👥 Work with a group. Describe a beautiful place in your city or town. Is it an old or new place? What can you see there? Who goes there? What do you like to do there?

Unit 6 Cities 93

Diana Reiss, Peter Gabriel, Neil Gershenfeld, and Vint Cerf
THE INTERSPECIES INTERNET? AN IDEA IN PROGRESS

Before You Watch

A Match the items to create complete sentences.

1. Communication is ____
2. The Internet is ____
3. The senses are ____
4. Species are ____

a. how a person or animal receives information about their environment.
b. a system of computer networks.
c. groups of animals that are similar.
d. using words, sounds, or signs to exchange information, thoughts, or feelings.

B Look at the words in the box. Choose the correct word to complete each sentence.

Word Bank
alien a creature from outer space
bonobo a rare, intelligent ape related to the chimpanzee
interact to communicate with
interface system linking two things
interplanetary between different planets
interspecies between different species
sentient a being capable of experiencing the world through its senses

1. A computer has an _____ to connect to the Internet.
2. Creatures that can think are called _____.
3. A creature from another world is called a(n) _____.
4. People from around the world _____ using the Internet.
5. Something that connects many planets is _____.

Diana Reiss, Peter Gabriel, Neil Gershenfeld, and Vint Cerf's idea worth spreading is that the Internet isn't just for humans—animals should have access too. Watch the full TED Talk at TED.com.

6. People and gorillas can communicate using _____ communication.
7. A _____ is a type of very intelligent ape.

C Can you think of a situation where people and animals communicate, or animals communicate with other animals? Can you think of a situation where you communicate with a machine? Discuss your ideas with a partner.

D You are going to watch a TED Talk about a new idea for an Interspecies Internet. Write down three things you think you will see in the video. Share your ideas with a partner.

_____
_____
_____

While You Watch

A Watch the TED Talk. Put the images on the next page in order. Write the number in the box.

B Write down two or three ideas from each speaker. After the TED Talk, discuss the ideas with a partner.

_____
_____

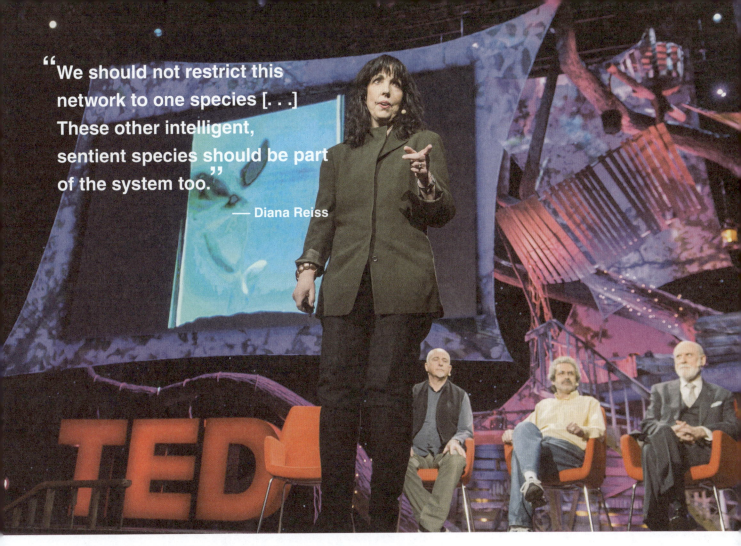

"We should not restrict this network to one species [...] These other intelligent, sentient species should be part of the system too."
— Diana Reiss

☐ "We thought, perhaps the most amazing tool that man's created is the Internet, and what would happen if we could somehow find new interfaces, visual-audio interfaces that would allow these remarkable sentient beings that we share the planet with access?"

☐ "I work with a lot of musicians from around the world, and often we don't have any common language at all, but we sit down behind our instruments, and suddenly there's a way for us to connect."

☐ "We participate in the Apps for Apes program Orangutan Outreach, and we use iPads to help stimulate and enrich the animals."

☐ "Now, there is a project that's underway called the Interplanetary Internet . . . What we're learning with these interactions with other species will teach us, ultimately, how we might interact with an alien from another world."

Diana Reiss, Peter Gabriel, Neil Gershenfeld, and Vint Cerf
THE INTERSPECIES INTERNET? AN IDEA IN PROGRESS

C ▶ Watch the TED Talk again. Match each speaker with the correct description.

1. ____ Peter Gabriel
2. ____ Neil Gershenfeld
3. ____ Vint Cerf
4. ____ Diana Reiss

a. He thinks that the Interspecies Internet can also be used to communicate with life on other planets.
b. He showed how the Interspecies Internet can work by video conferencing with animals.
c. She showed that dolphins can recognize themselves.
d. He played music with a bonobo.

After You Watch

A Read the list of ideas presented by the TED speakers. Then work with a partner to make two predictions for each idea.

Ideas	Predictions
1. communicating with other species using music	a. b.
2. the Interspecies Internet	a. b.
3. the Internet of Things	a. b.
4. the Interplanetary Internet	a. b.
5. communication with aliens	a. b.

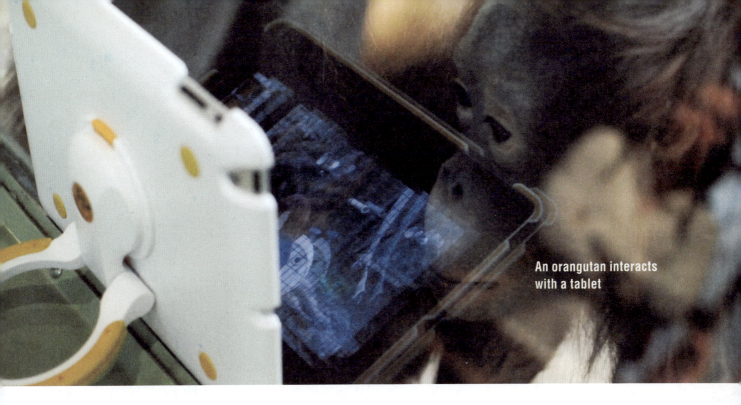

An orangutan interacts with a tablet

B Get together with another pair. Take turns sharing your predictions from Exercise **A**. Explain which of the outcomes you find most interesting and why. Share your ideas with the class.

C Think about how *you* communicate. Read the list of modes of communication below. Then, with a group, talk about which are the two best and worst ways to communicate with friends. Why?

e-mail	text message	in person
social media	letter	phone
letter	video conferencing	

D With your group, imagine that you are going to communicate with the following animals. How does each animal communicate? Why does each animal communicate? Do you think you would be able to communicate with each one? If so, how? Share your ideas with the class.

bonobo	elephant
dolphin	orangutan
dog	cat
parrot	bee

Challenge! Diana Reiss has been doing experiments with dolphins since her first dolphin-keyboard experiment in the 1980s. Read more about her at TED.com. Find her TED Talk "Thinking Dolphin" online. With a partner, pick one more part of her work to share with the class. Do more research if needed.

UNIT 7
Consequences

Melting water from a glacier flows over a waterfall in Iceland.

Look at the photo, then answer the questions:

1. What does this photo show?
2. What is the cause and effect demonstrated by this photo?

UNIT 7 GOALS

1. Talk about managing your money
2. Make choices on how to spend your money
3. Talk about cause and effect
4. Evaluate money and happiness

A GOAL 1: Talk About Managing Your Money

Vocabulary

A 🔊1 Listen to the passage. Fill in the blanks.

STUDENT LIFE

MANAGE YOUR MONEY

Congratulations! You have received your first student loan. How are you going to spend it? Are you going to go out and buy that new cell phone or those cool sneakers? Well, don't!

Before you spend a penny, you have to make a _____ and plan your spending. First, write down your _____ —how much money you receive. Then calculate your _____ (rent, transportation, food). If your _____ are lower than your income you are on the right track! Now you know how much money you have left to spend each month. But don't _____ or you will have to _____ money. Borrowing money from the bank is expensive. _____ are high. You could check to see if a friend or family member can _____ you the money.

You also have to think about the long term. How are you going to pay for that spring break at the beach, or buy your family presents? You will have to _____ some money every month. So, that new cell phone can wait. Manage your money and maybe you'll be able to take that spring break at the beach—in Mexico!

Word Focus

student loan money that the government lends to students

B Write the words you filled in the blanks of Exercise **A** next to the correct meanings.

1. the amount of money you spend _____
2. to ask someone to give you money _____
3. the amount of money you receive _____
4. to spend too much money _____
5. a spending plan _____
6. to give someone money _____
7. to put money in the bank for the future _____
8. the percentage (%) charged when you borrow money _____

C 🗣 Talk about how you manage your money with a partner. Use the words in Exercise **B**.

Conversation

A 🔊 2 Listen to the conversation. Choose the correct answer.

1. a. To take a vacation.
   b. To buy a new camera.
   c. To take vacation photos.
   d. Both a and b.

2. a. He doesn't have money to take a vacation.
   b. He can't afford a new camera.
   c. He can't decide whether to take a vacation or buy a new camera.
   d. He doesn't want to take a vacation.

B 🔊 2 Listen to the conversation again and fill in the blanks.

Jim: I don't know what to do. I want to _____, and I also want to buy a new _____.

Dave: I see. If you buy the _____, you won't have money _____. Is that it?

Jim: _____.

Dave: So, just take the _____. Don't buy the _____.

Jim: But if I don't buy the _____, I won't be able to take any _____ photos.

Dave: OK, just buy the _____.

Jim: But if I buy the _____, I won't be able to take the _____. And I won't need a camera.

Dave: Hmm…you have a problem.

C Practice the conversation with a partner. Switch roles and practice it again.

D Use the words in the box to make a new conversation.

E GOAL CHECK ✓ **Talk about managing your money**

Work with a partner. Discuss how you manage your money. What are your expenses? Do you have a budget? Do you save?

> **Real Language**
>
> *to get* sometimes means *to understand*
> (Do you) get it? = Do you understand?
> You got it! = You understood.
> I don't get you/it. = I don't understand you/it.

> binoculars   bird watching
> weekend   glasses
> movies   bicycle
> cycling tour

B GOAL 2: Make Choices on How to Spend Your Money

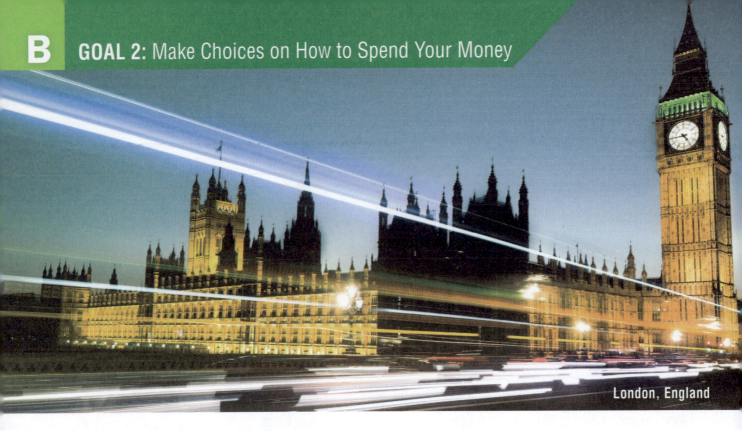

London, England

Listening

A 🔊 3 Listen to the conversation. Choose the correct answer.

1. a. London.   b. Paris.   c. Lyon.   d. New York.
2. a. Only one. b. Two.   c. Three.   d. Four.

B 🔊 3 Listen to the conversation again and answer the questions.

1. Is this the first time that the woman has visited England? _____
2. Why doesn't she want to take the plane? _____
3. Why doesn't she want to rent a car? _____
4. How long does it take to go from Paris to London by train? _____
5. How much does the train ticket cost? _____

Pronunciation: Intonation

A 🔊 4 Listen to the sentences. Draw the arrows to show rise or fall.

1. If I buy a car↗, I won't be able to pay the rent↘.
2. If you take the bus, it will be cheaper.
3. If we borrow some money, we will repay it in a month.
4. If Sara leaves now, she will catch the seven o'clock train.
5. If we take the plane, it will be quicker.

B 🔊 4 Listen again and repeat the sentences.

Communication

A Work with a partner. Plan a six-day visit to California. Each of you has $300 to spend on transportation. You will arrive in Los Angeles. You would like to visit Yosemite National Park, San Diego, and San Francisco.

> If we take the train, will it be cheaper?

> If we take the plane, it will be quicker.

> If we take the bus, it will be cheaper.

Yosemite National Park

	San Diego	San Francisco	Merced (for Yosemite)
Los Angeles	🚌 $40, 4 hours 🚆 $80, 3 hours ✈ $130, 1 hour	🚌 $60, 6 hours 🚆 $70, 8 hours (3 changes) ✈ $130, 1½ hours	🚌 $80, 7 hours 🚆 No service ✈ No service
San Diego		🚌 $135 return, 12 hours 🚆 No service ✈ $250, 1½ hours	🚌 $90, 10 hours 🚆 No service ✈ No service
San Francisco			🚌 $70, 4 hours 🚆 $60, 3 hours ✈ No service

	Itinerary	Transportation	Transportation costs
Day 1			
Day 2			
Day 3			
Day 4			
Day 5			
Day 6			

B **GOAL CHECK** ✓ **Make choices on how to spend your money**

Join another pair of students and explain to them how you decided to spend your transportation money.

Unit 7 Consequences

C GOAL 3: Talk About Cause and Effect

Language Expansion: Animal habitats

A Match the animals with their habitats.

▲ desert

▲ mountains

▲ monkey

▲ camel

▲ grasslands

▲ rain forest

▲ shark

▲ mountain goat

▲ coral reef

▲ elephant

B Complete the sentences. Use the habitats and animals in Exercise **A**.

1. Many countries near the equator have _____. They contain hundreds of different plants and animals, for example _____ and colorful birds.

2. _____ can live without water for many days. They are perfectly adapted to live in the _____.

3. The Great Barrier Reef in Australia is the biggest _____ in the world. It is the home of _____ and many other kinds of fish.

4. Kenya is famous for its _____. Tourists come from all over the world to see the animals, like lions and _____.

5. The highest _____ in the world are in Nepal. Not many animals live there. If you are lucky, you might see a _____.

Word Focus

habitat the place where a plant or animal normally lives

▲ Habitat destruction in a rain forest. Why is it important to save habitats like this?

Conversation

A 🔊 5 Listen to the conversation. Choose the correct answer.

1. a. Her car.   b. Habitat destruction.
   c. Climate change.   d. Her work.

2. a. Less money.   b. Less pollution.
   c. Less climate change. d. Less gasoline.

B 🔊 5 Listen to the conversation again and fill in the blanks.

Aya: I'm worried about all we hear and read about _____. It's important, but how can I help?

Sharon: _____, right?

Aya: Yes.

Sharon: It will help _____.

Aya: How will that help?

Sharon: Buses _____ lots of people. That _____ less gasoline is used per person. _____, right?

Aya: Yes, and I _____.

Sharon: Right!

C 🔄 Practice the conversation with a partner. Switch roles and practice it again.

D 🔄 **GOAL CHECK** ✓ **Talk about cause and effect**

Work with a partner. Choose an important problem or environmental issue. Make a list of the things you can do to help. Tell your partner what positive consequences your actions will have.

Real Language

You can say *right?* (rising tone) at the end of a statement to check information.
You can also use *right* (falling tone) to show you agree.

Unit 7 Consequences 105

D GOAL 4: Evaluate Money and Happiness

Listening

A Make a check mark (✓) next to the items that describe spending money. Discuss with a partner about which activities make you feel best.

1. _____ buying clothes for yourself
2. _____ spending time with a friend
3. _____ reading a book
4. _____ buying a present for someone in your family
5. _____ donating to a charity
6. _____ going out to eat

B 6 Listen to the passage. Circle **T** for *true* or **F** for *false*.

1. Many people believe that winning the lottery will make them happy.   T   F
2. People that win the lottery never have problem with money.   T   F
3. Michael Norton has done experiments to test how people feel after exercising.   T   F
4. Michael Norton's experiments show that spending money on others makes people happy.   T   F

C 6 Listen to the passage again and answer the questions.

1. Who is Michael Norton?
   _____

2. What is he interested in?
   _____

3. What does the example about lottery winners show?
   _____

4. What are Norton's experiments about?
   _____

Word Focus

conflict problem
debt money that has to be paid
experiment test
lottery game of chance with cash prize
research exploitation, investigation

"Maybe the reason that money doesn't make us happy is that we're always spending it on the wrong things."

— Michael Norton

D GOAL 4: Evaluate Money and Happiness

Communication

A You won $100 in the lottery. Write down five possible ways to use the money.

B Discuss your ideas with a partner. Talk about each way to use money and discuss any differences.

C GOAL CHECK ✓ **Evaluate money and happiness**

Work together to decide how to use the money. How much will you spend and what will you buy? Will you save or give away any of the money? What might happen as a result of how you spend the money?

How you spend your money has an effect on your happiness.

Mount Kilimanjaro

VIDEO JOURNAL: The Missing Snows of Kilimanjaro E

Before You Watch

A Read the chain of actions and consequences. Number the sentences below to make a similar chain.

Cars and airplanes produce carbon dioxide. > Carbon dioxide makes the atmosphere hotter. > The glaciers of Kilimanjaro melt.

____ Kilimanjaro's glaciers get smaller.   _1_ People cut down trees.

____ There is less water in the atmosphere.   ____ There is less rain and snow.

B Write the meaning of the words with the help of a dictionary.

continent: _____

Tanzania: _____

Cairo: _____

Cape Town: _____

equator: _____

tropical: _____

peak: _____

majestic: _____

glacier: _____

ice cap: _____

> **Word Focus**
>
> **deforestation** when trees and forests are cut down
>
> **to melt** to change from ice to water

Unit 7 Consequences 109

E VIDEO JOURNAL: The Missing Snows of Kilimanjaro

While You Watch

A Watch the video. Fill in the numbers and dates.

1. Kilimanjaro is nearly _____ miles high.
2. It is around _____ miles south of the equator.
3. The glaciers on Kilimanjaro are _____ years old.
4. Experts think that the glaciers could disappear by the year _____.

B Watch the video again and choose the correct answer.

1. Where is Mount Kilimanjaro located?
   a. Africa. b. Asia. c. Europe. d. North America.

2. What is attractive about Mount Kilimanjaro for visitors?
   a. Its height. b. Its peaks. c. Its width. d. Its climate.

3. Why is the ice cap important to local habitants?
   a. It's amazing to see. b. It's excellent farming land.
   c. It's an important source of water. d. It has a long history.

4. What is NOT a possible reason for the melting Kilimanjaro's glaciers?
   a. Climate change. b. Global warming.
   c. Deforestation. d. Excessive farming.

5. The disappearance of Kilimanjaro's glaciers might cause the following problems EXCEPT _____.
   a. no source of water for people living on or near the mountain
   b. fewer tourists
   c. less money
   d. less farming land

After You Watch

A Discuss the question with a partner: Is there anything that you can do to stop the melting of Kilimanjaro's glaciers?

Communication

A Use "if" structure to talk about the consequences of people failing to protect the environment. The following sentences can serve as examples.

1. If we continue to burn fossil fuels, the climate will change.
2. We will lose many valuable animals if we destroy their habitats.

FURTHER PRACTICE: *Enjoy a Nature Vacation!* F

Listening

A 🔊 7 Listen to the passage. Answer the questions.

1. How many places are mentioned in the passage?
   _____

2. How will people get to a new airport near the Rainforest Hotel?
   _____

3. How many people can a Coral Reef Ship accommodate?
   _____

B 🔊 7 Listen to the passage again and choose the correct answers. There might be more than one correct.

1. In which one of the following will guests learn about the environment?
   - a. Rainforest Hotel.
   - b. Coral Reef Ship.
   - c. Mountain Camp.
   - d. None.

2. In which one will people see fish?
   - a. Rainforest Hotel.
   - b. Coral Reef Ship.
   - c. Mountain Camp.
   - d. None.

3. Which one can accommodate the most people?
   - a. Rainforest Hotel.
   - b. Coral Reef Ship.
   - c. Mountain Camp.
   - d. None.

4. In which one will guests go walking?
   - a. Rainforest Hotel.
   - b. Coral Reef Ship.
   - c. Mountain Camp.
   - d. None.

5. In which one will people eat local food from this place?
   - a. Rainforest Hotel.
   - b. Coral Reef Ship.
   - c. Mountain Camp.
   - d. None.

6. In which one will people buy things from this place?
   - a. Rainforest Hotel.
   - b. Coral Reef Ship.
   - c. Mountain Camp.
   - d. None.

C Discuss with a partner about which of the places in Exercise **B** is the worst and which is the best for the environment. Explain your answers. Use sentences with " if " to talk about consequences.

Unit 7 Consequences 111

UNIT 8 Challenges

Ford Ironman World Championship at Kailua Bay in Kona, Hawaii

Look at the photo, then answer the questions:

1. What phrase best describes the picture?
2. What do you think of when you hear the word *challenge*?

UNIT 8 GOALS

1. Talk about facing challenges
2. Discuss past accomplishments
3. Talk about abilities
4. Describe a personal challenge

A GOAL 1: Talk About Facing Challenges

▲ A young girl plays the stringed koto.

Word Focus

To face a challenge means to decide to do something new and difficult.

Word Focus

To **make progress** means to improve or get nearer to a goal over time.

Vocabulary

A 🔊 1 Listen to the passage. Fill in the blanks.

The word "challenge" might make you think of _____ activities like playing sports. But _____ activities such as learning a new language or a new _____ can also be a challenge. For me, learning to play a _____ instrument is a challenge, but also an _____. You might feel afraid to try it, but it is as exciting as traveling to a new place, and the only _____ you need is a violin, a guitar, or in my case — a koto.

When I started my koto lessons, my _____ was to learn to play this _____ instrument well enough to play for my family. Now, I am making good _____ with the help of my music teacher. She thinks I'm getting better every week! I can probably _____ my goal soon, and then I'll play the koto at my father's birthday party.

B Write the words you filled in the blanks of Exercise **A** next to the correct meanings.

1. related to the body _____
2. related to music _____
3. improvement _____
4. things needed for an activity _____
5. unusual and exciting activity _____
6. succeed in making something happen _____
7. related to the mind _____
8. something you hope to do over time _____
9. activity that requires special knowledge _____
10. surprising, interesting, and wonderful _____

C Tell a partner what the word "challenge" means to you. In a group, discuss what you would do to deal with the challenges you face.

Conversation

A 🔊 2 Listen to the conversation. Choose the correct answer.

1. a. Their biggest challenges.   b. Their hobbies.
   c. Their vacation.   d. Their living style.
2. a. Getting a scholarship.   b. Getting money from her boss.
   c. Getting the driver's license.   d. Getting used to a new school.

B 🔊 2 Listen to the conversation again and fill in the blanks.

Helen: What was the _____ thing you did last year?

Paul: Do you mean the _____ thing?

Helen: No, I mean your _____ challenge.

Paul: Well, _____ a new school when my family moved was a challenge.

Helen: For me, getting my _____ was a challenge. It was hard!

C Practice the conversation with a partner. What was difficult about each challenge?

D GOAL CHECK ✓ **Talk about facing challenges**

Talk about a challenge you have faced with a partner. What was happening in your life at that time? How did the challenge change your life, or change you?

B GOAL 2: Discuss Past Accomplishments

Word Focus

endangered If an animal is *endangered*, its population is so small that it may die out.

▲ Jenny Daltry, herpetologist and explorer

Engage!

How do you feel about crocodiles and snakes? Is it important to protect *unpopular* endangered animals?

Listening

A What do you know about these endangered animals? Which animal do you think people should work the hardest to save? Why?

▲ giant panda

▲ Siamese crocodile

▲ Antiguan racer (snake)

▲ Humboldt penguin

B 🔊 3 Listen to the interview of Jenny Daltry. Choose the correct answer.

1. a. She discovered a group of Siamese crocodiles.
   b. She found a new kind of bird in Cambodia.
   c. She helped scientists protect panda bears.
   d. She saved a new kind of bear in Cambodia.

2. a. Walking through marshes.
   b. Avoiding dangerous snakes.
   c. Educating people about crocodiles.
   d. Raising money for these endangered animals.

3. a. She explained that crocodiles are important to the marshes.
   b. She explained that crocodiles are not really dangerous.
   c. She explained that crocodiles are extinct.
   d. She explained many endangered animals to people.

C 🔊 3 Listen to the interview again and answer the questions.

1. How many crocodiles are in the largest group? _____

2. How many acres are now protected by the government? _____

3. How do most people feel about crocodiles? _____
   _____

4. What was Daltry doing when she found out about the Antiguan racer snake?
   _____

Pronunciation: Words that end in -ed

A 🔊 4 Listen to these words that end in -ed. The -ed is pronounced in three different ways.

/t/	/d/	/ɪd/
help helped	listen listened	start started

B 🔊 5 Listen, repeat, and check (✓) the column of the sound you hear.

Present tense	Simple past tense	-ed ending sound		
		/t/	/d/	/ɪd/
walk	walked	___	___	___
protect	protected	___	___	___
cross	crossed	___	___	___
discover	discovered	___	___	___
climb	climbed	___	___	___
start	started	___	___	___
need	needed	___	___	___
close	closed	___	___	___

C Write down ten verbs in the present tense. Some verbs should end in *t* or *d*. Say one of your words and ask your partner to say it in the past tense. Then switch roles.

Communication

A With a partner, make a list of challenges that people of your age face.

	Challenges that people of our age face
1.	
2.	
3.	

B Get together with another pair of students and compare your lists. Try to agree on the two or three most difficult challenges for people of your age.

C **GOAL CHECK** ✓ **Discuss past accomplishments**

Write two or three sentences about a famous person or a person you know. Choose from the list below or use your own idea. What challenges did he or she face in the past? How did the person achieve his or her goal? Tell your partner about the person you chose.

scientist or explorer   writer or artist   political figure   businessperson

Word Focus

To **achieve a goal** means to succeed in doing something you hoped to do.

C GOAL 3: Talk About Abilities

Language Expansion: Phrasal verbs

A Match each phrasal verb with its meaning.

1. set out _____
2. give up _____
3. watch out _____
4. grow up _____
5. keep on _____
6. run out of _____
7. put up with _____
8. break down _____

a. accept something bad without being upset
b. grow from a child to an adult
c. finish the amount of something that you have
d. leave on a trip
e. be very careful
f. stop trying
g. continue trying
h. stop working

Word Focus

Phrasal verbs are two- or three-word combinations that have a special meaning.

set + out leave on a trip

B 🔊 6 Listen to this passage. Choose the correct answer.

1. a. 14.
   c. 4.
   b. 40.
   d. 44.

2. a. To sail from Tokyo to France.
   b. To sail from England to Tokyo.
   c. To sail from Tokyo to Francisco.
   d. To sail from Francisco to Tokyo.

3. a. On July 20.
   b. On July 22.
   c. On July 24.
   d. On July 28.

4. a. Because it was snowing at night.
   b. Because it was storming at night.
   c. Because it was too dark at night.
   d. Because it was raining at night.

5. a. The Atlantic Ocean.
   b. The Pacific Ocean.
   c. The Indian Ocean.
   d. The Arctic Ocean.

Engage!

What do you think about Subaru's parents? Was he really old enough to set out alone?

▲ Subaru Takahashi, the youngest person to sail alone across the Pacific Ocean

Conversation

A 🔊 7 Listen to the conversation. Choose the correct answer.

1. a. To climb a mountain.   b. To join a club.
   c. To ride a bike.   d. To play basketball with her friends.
2. a. Jogging.   b. Racing.
   c. Hiking.   d. Skiing.

B 🔊 7 Listen to the conversation again and fill in the blanks.

Lisa: Do you know what I want to do next summer? My _____ is to climb Black Mountain.

Mari: Are you _____? Black Mountain is too hard to climb. Don't you need special _____?

Lisa: I already asked about it. I just need _____.

Mari: And you are not strong enough to climb a mountain!

Lisa: You're right, I can't do it now. But I'll _____ every weekend. Next summer, I will be _____ enough to climb the mountain.

Mari: Well, I like _____. I will go with you sometimes.

> swim across a lake
> travel to ____ (another country)
> take a *karate* class

C Practice the conversation with a partner. Then have new conversations about the activities in the box.

D GOAL CHECK ✓ **Talk about abilities**

Write down six things you want to do. Discuss whether you can do these things now. Are you old enough to do them? Are they affordable or too expensive?

Unit 8 Challenges 119

D GOAL 4: Describe a Personal Challenge

For Your Information
The North Pole

The North Pole is the northernmost point on Earth. It lies in the middle of the Arctic Ocean, on sea ice above salt water that is 4,261 meters (13,980 feet) deep. Because the ice is constantly moving, it's impossible to build permanent scientific stations, such as those at the South Pole.

Surprisingly, it is not known for certain who first discovered the North Pole. The American explorer Frederick Cook claimed he reached it on April 21, 1908, but his only companions were two Inuit men who had no knowledge of science or navigation. Another American, Robert Peary, said he reached the Pole on April 6, 1909, but his navigational calculations were widely disbelieved. Most surprising of all, the first person proved to have actually seen the North Pole, Roald Amundsen, did it from an airship in 1926. He was also the first explorer to reach the *South Pole, in 1912!*

Word Focus

float to rest on top of water

tent portable shelter

grab to take suddenly

waterproof does not allow water to get in

GPS global positioning system

Listening

A What do you know about the Arctic? Choose the correct answer.

1. In the winter in the Arctic, it's dark _____ hours every day.
   a. 12   b. 20   c. 24
2. The North Pole is on _____.
   a. land   b. water   c. ice
3. In the Arctic, you can see _____.
   a. polar bears b. penguins   c. polar bears and penguins

B 🔊 8 Listen to the passage. Choose the correct answer.

1. a. On January 20.   b. On January 21.
   c. On January 22.   d. On January 24.
2. a. Skiing and climbing mountains.   b. Skiing and skating.
   c. Jogging and climbing mountains. d. Skating and riding bikes.
3. a. Because they were too energetic.
   b. Because a polar bear ripped their tent open.
   c. Because they were angry with each other.
   d. Because it was too cold there.
4. a. 3 or 4 times.   b. 4 or 5 times.
   c. 5 or 6 times.   d. 6 or 7 times.
5. a. Because Mike is a fast walker.
   b. Because Boerge was afraid to be the first one.
   c. Because Boerge was not stronger than Mike.
   d. Because Boerge had been to the pole before.

C 🔊 8 Listen to the passage again and answer the questions.

1. What was Boerge and Mike's idea?
   _____
2. How did Boerge and Mike travel?
   _____
3. How far did they go every day?
   _____
4. What happened when they were close to the Pole?
   _____
5. When did they get to the Pole?
   _____

ARCTIC DREAMS AND NIGHTMARES

Ousland and Horn at the North Pole

D GOAL 4: Describe a Personal Challenge

Communication

A Discuss the questions with a partner.

1. People face challenges for different reasons, but there is usually some reward when we accomplish our goal. What are three or four challenges in life that cannot be avoided? (For example, it can be a challenge to get along well with all of our family members or neighbors.) What are the rewards if we face those challenges?

2. Tell your partner about two or three challenges in your life that you chose for yourself. Why did you choose to do those things?

B GOAL CHECK ✓ **Describe a personal challenge**

Describe a challenging experience from your own life to your partner. You can use the topic sentence below, and add some interesting details to make your story complete.

Topic sentence: When I was … years old, I decided to …

Details: It was a challenge because …

VIDEO JOURNAL: *Searching for the Snow Leopard* E

Snow Leopard running after prey

Before You Watch

A Read the following sentences. Choose the one that is closest in meaning to the underlined word.

1. It was the hardest story I'd ever done physically because of the <u>altitude</u> and steepness of the mountains.
   - **a.** height
   - **b.** latitude
   - **c.** attitude
   - **d.** longitude

2. Many snow leopards have been <u>spotted</u> as high as 18,000 feet and they're notoriously camera shy.
   - **a.** spitted
   - **b.** killed
   - **c.** trapped
   - **d.** seen

3. We will be here a few days to <u>acclimate</u> to the altitudes at 12,000 feet.
   - **a.** climb
   - **b.** adapt
   - **c.** claim
   - **d.** adopt

4. Once we knew we were having success in a specific <u>trail</u> then I "mined" that with cameras.
   - **a.** tail
   - **b.** trial
   - **c.** track
   - **d.** location

5. Snow leopards often go to hunt wherever they find the scent of their <u>prey</u>.
   - **a.** pray
   - **b.** animals or birds
   - **c.** hunters
   - **d.** flash

B Fill in each blank with a word from the box. Use your dictionary to help you.

| altitudes | camera shy | hunts | prey | trails |

The snow leopard lives at high _____ in the mountains of Central Asia. There, the leopard _____ its _____: animals such as mountain goats and sheep. Snow leopards are _____ and few people have photographed them. For photographer Steve Winter, getting good pictures in these cold mountains was a physical and mental challenge. He and his team set up cameras on _____ where the leopards walk. Then they watched and waited.

For Your Information
Snow Leopards

The snow leopard can survive in the cold, snowy mountains of Central Asia thanks to thick insulating fur and wide, fur-covered feet that allow them to walk more easily on the snow. They have strong legs for jumping and use their long tails for balance and as blankets to protect themselves from the cold. However, the number of snow leopards left in the wild is diminishing. They are sometimes killed by herders of sheep and goat because they prey on their animals. They are hunted illegally for their fur and for their organs, which are used in traditional Chinese medicine. In addition to this, their habitat is vanishing. As a result of these threats to their survival, conservationists are working hard to protect this rare and beautiful animal.

Unit 8 Challenges 123

E VIDEO JOURNAL: Searching for the Snow Leopard

While You Watch

A ▶ Watch the video. Check (✓) the activities in the left box you see in the video.

- ☐ driving on mountain roads
- ☐ cooking in a tent
- ☐ riding on horses
- ☐ fixing broken equipment
- ☐ touching a leopard
- ☐ setting up cameras

B ▶ Watch the video again and choose the correct answer.

1. How many frames did Steve Winter shoot in pursuit of the elusive snow leopard?
   a. More than 13,000 frames.　　b. More than 3,000 frames.
   c. More than 1,300 frames.　　d. More than 30,000 frames.

2. Why did Steve Winter regard searching for the snow leopard as the hardest thing?
   a. Because of the danger from the snow leopard.
   b. Because of the altitude and steepness of the mountains.
   c. Because of the shortage of money.
   d. Because of the opposition from the government.

3. How many snow leopards exist in the wild according to the narrator?
   a. About 5,300.　　b. About 5,500.　　c. About 3,500.　　d. About 3,300.

4. How does the cat appear in the first image?
   a. Dangerous.　　b. Curious.　　c. Calm.　　d. Shy.

5. Why does the snow leopard have a long tail?
   a. The long tail helps the snow leopard keep its balance.
   b. The long tail can kill the prey directly.
   c. The long tail can help the snow leopard swim.
   d. The long tail makes snow leopard more attractive.

After You Watch

A Do you think Steve Winter got a lot of pictures of snow leopards? Why do you think Winter and his team decided to do such a difficult project? Discuss these questions with your class.

Communication

A If you decide to observe rare animals in a remote area, what preparations do you think you would need? Talk with a partner about the preparations. Write them down.

	Preparations
1.	I will take a camera with me in order to take pictures of some rare animals.
2.	
3.	
4.	
5.	

FURTHER PRACTICE: *How Do You Spell...* F

Listening

A 🔊 9 Listen to the passage. Circle **T** for *true* or **F** for *false*.

1. Sameer didn't make any mistakes in the spelling bee.   T   F
2. The words in a spelling bee are words that we use every day.   T   F
3. You can see a spelling bee on television.   T   F
4. Students prepare for a long time before the National Spelling Bee.   T   F
5. Sameer's family helped him before the spelling bee.   T   F
6. Sameer won a violin and computer games in the National Spelling Bee.   T   F

B 🔊 9 Listen to the passage again and choose the correct answer.

1. How old was Sameer when he wanted to become the best speller and win the National Spelling Bee?
   - **a.** 10.
   - **b.** 13.
   - **c.** 20.
   - **d.** 30.

2. What is a spelling bee?
   - **a.** A spelling contest for college students.
   - **b.** A spelling contest for middle school students.
   - **c.** A spelling contest for elementary school students.
   - **d.** A spelling contest for all students.

3. How many students entered the National Spelling Bee in that year?
   - **a.** 218.
   - **b.** 228.
   - **c.** 280.
   - **d.** 288.

4. How much money did Sameer win in the Spelling Bee?
   - **a.** $14,000.
   - **b.** $44,000.
   - **c.** $40,000.
   - **d.** $48,000.

5. Besides spelling, what other interests does Sameer have?
   - **a.** Playing the violin and enjoying video games.
   - **b.** Playing the violin and enjoying reading.
   - **c.** Playing the violin and watching TV.
   - **d.** Playing basketball and enjoying video games.

C 🔊 9 Listen to the passage once more and fill in the blanks.

A spelling bee is a contest for _____ students who speak English. They have to _____ difficult words. All the students stand up. The teacher says a _____. The first student has to _____ it. If the student spells the word wrong, he or she _____. At the end of the spelling bee, the winner is the _____ student who is standing. There are spelling bees for schools, _____, and states. Every year, there is the big National Spelling Bee in the city of _____. This year, the _____ was Sameer Mishra. He studied the dictionary for _____ hours every day!

Unit 1 Moving Forward

TEDTALKS

Michael Norton Professor/Psychologist
HOW TO BUY HAPPINESS

Before You Watch

A Read the list. Make a check (✓) next to the ways that you use money.

☐ pay bills
☐ buy things for yourself
☐ save money
☐ eat at a restaurant
☐ buy gifts for others
☐ spend money on expenses
☐ donate (give away) money
☐ lend money to others

B Read the sentences. Match the word in **bold** to its meaning.

a. give someone a reason to do something	d. helps others
b. good effect	e. money spent for a future reward
c. payment that is received	f. scientific test
	g. how well you work

1. If I don't sleep enough, I don't **perform** well at school. ____

2. I like to get good grades in school; it **motivates** me to study. ____

3. Alexandra decided to make an **investment** with her extra money. ____

4. The **return** on the investment was small, only 20 dollars. ____

5. Jack is working on an **experiment** about sunlight. ____

6. Exercise has many **benefits**, such as being healthy. ____

7. Being a volunteer is a **prosocial** activity. ____

Michael Norton's idea worth spreading is that money can buy happiness! What matters isn't how much you have, but how you spend it. Watch Norton's full TED Talk on TED.com.

C You are going to watch a TED Talk about Michael Norton's experiments on how money makes people feel. What types of experiments do you think you will see? Talk about your ideas with a partner. Look at the list in Exercise **A** for ideas.

While You Watch

A Watch the TED Talk. Complete the missing information in the chart as you watch.

Experiment	How much money	Spent money on themselves	Spent money on others
	5 or ____ dollars	did not feel happier	
sales teams			sold more
dodgeball teams	did not say		won more games

B Read the photo captions on the next page. What quotes are you surprised by? Place a check (✓) next to the captions that you are surprised by. Then, in small groups, talk about why you are surprised.

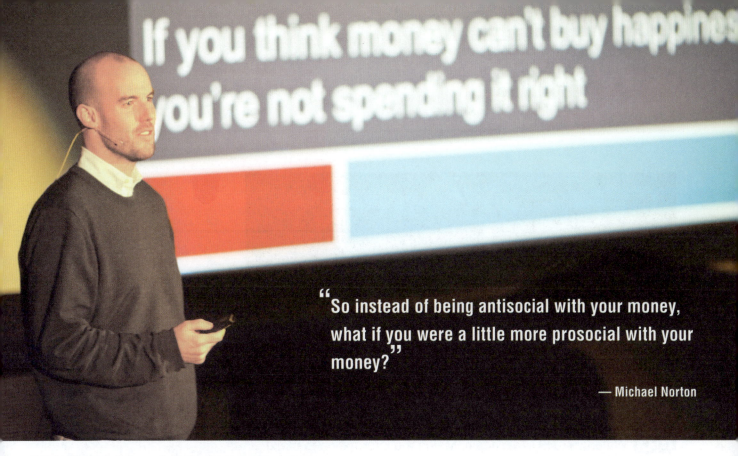

> "So instead of being antisocial with your money, what if you were a little more prosocial with your money?"
>
> — Michael Norton

☐ "In fact, it doesn't matter how much money you spent. What really matters is that you spent it on somebody else rather than on yourself."

☐ "People who spent money on other people got happier. People who spent money on themselves, nothing happened."

Listen for Key Information

As you listen, you do not need to focus on every word you hear. Listen for specific words and phrases to get the information you need.

☐ "One of the teams pooled their money and bought a piñata . . . very silly, trivial thing to do, but think of the difference on a team that didn't do that at all."

☐ "The teams that we give the money to spend on each other, they become different teams and, in fact, they dominate the league by the time they're done."

☐ "And so I'll just say, I think if you think money can't buy happiness you're not spending it right."

TEDTALKS **127**

Michael Norton Professor/Psychologist
HOW TO BUY HAPPINESS

This boy is buying food for his family. How do you think he feels?

C ▶ Watch the TED Talk again. Match the information to make sentences about what Michael Norton's experiments suggest.

1. ____ If people on sports teams spend money on themselves,
2. ____ If students spend money on each other,
3. ____ If people on sales teams spend money on each other,
4. ____ If students spend money on themselves,
5. ____ If people on sales teams spend money on themselves,
6. ____ If people on sports teams spend money on each other,

a. they will feel happier.
b. they will not sell more.
c. they will win more games.
d. they will sell more.
e. they will not feel happier.
f. they will not win more games.

After You Watch

A ▶ Complete these sentences.

1. To be prosocial with money means to spend it on _____.
2. People who are prosocial with money often feel _____ and perform _____ at work or at sports.
3. Norton suggests that it is not important how _____ money you spend on others; the benefits are the same.

B 🔄 Work with a partner. Take turns making statements about what you saw in the TED Talk. Your partner says which experiment you are talking about.

C 👥 Work with a group. Make a list of advice for a person who wants to have a happy and healthy lifestyle. Use what you already knew and what you learned in the TED Talk.

(You should . . .)   (You must not . . .)

D Interview three classmates about the last time they spent money on someone else. Follow the steps below.

- Write a list of questions, using *Who, What, How much,* and *Why.*

Questions	Names		
1.			
2.			
3.			
4.			
5.			

- Interview your classmates. Ask follow-up questions. Find out how your classmates felt after spending the money.
- Share what you learned with the class. Did what you learned from your classmates match what you learned in the TED Talk?

E With your group, look at the chart in Exercise **D**. Think about how you and your group spend money. Can you think of ways to spend money that are more prosocial? Think of a way to spend money that would be more prosocial and share your idea with the class.

Challenge! Place a check (✓) next to the four statements that represent the main ideas of Norton's talk.

____ Money cannot buy happiness.

____ Spending money in a prosocial way has a positive effect.

____ Spending money on others often makes people feel happier, be more productive, and have stronger relationships.

____ The important thing is to spend money on others—even a trivial amount can have a positive effect.

____ Winning money makes people happy.

____ The positive effects of spending money in a prosocial way seem to be the same all over the world.

____ People should not buy things for themselves.

With a team, pick one idea and talk about ways people can work toward using the idea in their own lives. Come up with a plan of action and share it with the class.